Antiracism, Culture and Social
Justice in Education

Antiracism, Culture and Social Justice in Education

Edited by
Morwenna Griffiths and Barry Troyna

tb

Trentham Books

First published in 1995 by Trentham Books Limited

Trentham Books Limited
Westview House
734 London Road
Oakhill
Stoke-on-Trent
Staffordshire
England ST4 5NP

© Morwenna Griffiths and Barry Troyna

British Cataloguing in Publication Data
A catalogue record for this book is available from the British Library.

ISBN: 1 85856 037 3

Designed and typeset by Trentham Print Design Ltd., Chester and printed in Great Britain by Bemrose Shafron (Printers) Ltd., Chester.

iv

Contents

Foreword

Jean Rudduck

I am very pleased that the British Educational Research Association (BERA) is associated with this book. There are two reasons: one is to do with the contributors and the other with the focus.

BERA has chosen to make support for new researchers a priority. By 'new researchers' we mean research students and people in their first research post. At the annual conference at Oxford in September, 1994, Donald McIntyre and his colleagues, who were responsible for the conference programme, broke new ground by organising a special strand for new researchers; this was repeated at the 1995 conference at Bath, and will, we hope, become a feature of subsequent conferences, with the new researchers themselves taking responsibility for determining the agenda for their sessions — but also participating in other conference sessions. We also hope to encourage, in partnership with departments of education in different parts of the country, other events for new researchers that will help them to feel that, although small in number and often scattered, they are part of a network that can offer professional and social support. BERA is also launching, in 1995, a competition for an outstanding student dissertation — and, as part of the award, we shall seek to arrange meetings between the author and appropriate publishing house and give the author· support in preparing the manuscript for possible publication.

It is particularly important at the present time that we recognise and respect the status of new researchers. The research assessment exercise is, unwittingly, in danger of marginalising them. The logical outcome of the current 'transfer market' (where departments seek to sign up, before the audit date of the next exercise, researchers with a string of prestigious publications and a dowry of externally funded research projects) is to increase the amount of money invested in senior staff — with the consequence that new researchers are likely to find fewer openings and resources to support them. BERA is concerned to keep high on the agenda the need to ensure a flow of high quality people who can take their place in the research community with commitment and confidence. Another side effect of the research selectivity exercise is that the favoured journals are all hanging up their 'No Vacancies' signs — they tend to be 'full' several editions ahead — and new researchers will find it difficult to jostle for space alongside experienced researchers. This book is making an important statement about new researchers: it is offering them visibility. We hope that other publishing houses and editors of educational journals will take heed and reflect on what they can do to provide openings for new researchers.

The focus of this book is clearly one that BERA would want to endorse. In 1995, Council chose, as the theme for the BERA symposium at the 1995 American Educational Association Research annual conference, 'Equity Issues in Education' (and the symposium team included established researchers and some who were nearer the beginning of their research career). In a competitive research climate it is tempting for researchers to seek out new territories and to allow their research agenda to be shaped by the priorities of funding agencies — which, at the moment, do not give particular prominence to the issues that this book is concerned with. To some extent we need to attend to the market in order to survive but at the same time we have to ensure that we are sustaining enquiry into the issues that the research community considers important even if our programmes of research are held together by little more than our own commitment and informal networks. But commitment and informal research partnerships have taken us a long way forward — as the chapters in this book demonstrate. Progress has also made us more aware of the enormity of the task — and how resolutely the habits of power relations hold injustice and inequity in place. We must continue to find ways of examining the social structures and institutional infrastructures that sustain inequity and we must continue to develop strategies for achieving a more widespread and authentic respect for diversity. Indeed the author of the first chapter calls for a sharper examination of the 'complex matrices of power relations' (she might have said, coining a word, 'the patrices of power relations').

It is encouraging to find that the voices in the book resonate so strongly with the voices being heard in the American Educational Research Association (AERA). William Russell, reviewing the role and emerging policy of AERA, argues that 'Ethnic and gender research and scholarship must be viewed as a valuable intellectual pursuit within AERA and academe not only for its substantive, cutting-edge contributions but also as a vehicle to attract students of colour to the community'. He comments on the 'tragically small' numbers of minority groups entering research and post secondary teaching as a career, and he goes on:

> The increased demand for knowledge and understanding about minorities and education ... demands a strong cadre of minority researchers who can and must contribute creative, nontraditional perspectives on what should be done in classrooms, schools, and curriculum inasmuch as traditional approaches have not sufficed. (1994, pp.27-28

Morwenna Griffiths and Barry Troyna are to be congratulated for bringing together some of those 'creative, non-traditional perspectives' in this book.

Jean Rudduck
President of BERA, 1994-5

Notes on contributors

Editors

Morwenna Griffiths lectures in Social Justice and Education in the School of Education at the University of Nottingham. Her latest books are *Feminisms and the Self: The Web of identity* (Routledge), and *In Fairness to Children: Social Justice in the Primary School* (David Fulton) with Carol Davies. She has published widely in the area of social justice and education.

Barry Troyna holds a personal readership and is Director of Research Development in the Institute of Education at Warwick University. He is editor of the *British Educational Research Journal* and a member of the editorial boards of the *Cambridge Journal of Education, Discourse*, and *Journal of Education Policy*. His latest books include *Racism and Education: Research Perspectives* (Open University Press) and *Researching Education Policy* (Falmer Press) with David Halpin.

Contributors

Ghazala Bhatti is Lecturer in the School of Education at the Open University. She has taught in both primary and secondary schools. She has also been involved in community education work. She was a Research Fellow in the Department of Educational Studies, University of Oxford. She has recently completed her doctorate at the Open University. It was based on studying the influence of home and school lives of Asian children. Her research interests include ethnicity and 'race', culture and social class.

Paul Connolly is currently Lecturer in Sociology, University of Ulster at Magee College. His research interests lie in the area of culture, ethnicity and identity, and especially in exploring the ways in which cultural identities are formed and reproduced within the articulation of discourses on 'race' and ethnicity, gender, class and age. He has published a number of articles and is currently writing a book, *Growing up in the Inner City: Racism, Cultural Identities and the Primary School* due to be published by the Open University Press in 1996.

Richard Hatcher is senior lecturer in the Faculty of Education at the University of Central England in Birmingham, and Director of Research in the Faculty. His particular interests include social inequality in education, education policy and politics, and the study of children's cultures.

Kaye Haw is completing her PhD at Nottingham University. She has taught in three comprehensive schools and in Higher Education. Her research is focused on the interaction of 'race' and gender with particular reference to Muslim girls, and she has published in the area. She is the mother of three young children and part-time researcher on two funded projects at Nottingham University.

Mehreen Mirza works in the Department of Public Policy in the University of Central Lancashire. She is currently completing some funded research in the area of 'race', gender and educational decision making in the North West of England. She is presently completing her doctorate.

Sarah Neal is a lecturer in the School of Sociology and Social Policy at Middlesex University. She is currently completing ESRC- funded doctoral research on equal opportunities and antiracism in Higher Education. Her academic interests have been consistently drawn to the issues of social division, inequality and oppression in contemporary Britain, particularly in terms of 'race' and gender. She sees her research interests as continuing to be influenced by the issues of 'race', racism and gender in the constantly shifting contexts of contemporary Britain.

Lynne Raphael Reed began her career as a social policy researcher before training as a teacher and working for ten years in Inner London secondary schools, mainly in the East End. She joined the Faculty of Education at the University of the West of England, Bristol, in 1990 as a senior lecturer in Educational Policy Studies. Since then she has worked across initial and inservice courses for teachers and is the co-ordinator of the Masters' programme in the Faculty.

Tony Sewell was born in London where he now lives. He has published two books, *Garvey's Children: the legacy of Marcus Garvey* and a novel called *Jamaica Inc.* He is a regular columnist in the *Voice* newspaper and has a radio phone-in show on Choice FM radio. He is currently completing his PhD in the Education Faculty at Nottingham University. His research interests are gender, 'race', special needs and American education.

Claudette Williams has a particular interest in Early Years education and in the education of African Caribbean children. She taught nursery and infant children for many years. She now lectures at the University of North London.

Introduction

Morwenna Griffiths and Barry Troyna

This book collects together a variety of new perspectives on the related issues of antiracism, culture and social justice in Britain. It provides a platform for a number of new voices, and brings a spotlight to bear on recent data and fresh ideas in an area which is in great need of updating and renewal. After all, not only has research in the area of racism, social justice and education been relatively underfunded in recent years, but also this area is marked by continuing change and metamorphosis. This collection of research, then, brings together emerging material which will, we hope, engage readers into reassessing their own theoretical understanding, their politics and their practice.

The set of contributions has been brought together in the expectation that its readers will come from a variety of educational settings, so we envision that they have a number of different reasons for reading it. They should be able to draw from the collection what is relevant and interesting, whatever kind of institution they work in, and whatever their reason for interest in antiracism, culture and social justice. All the chapters are written for this wide range of audience and make no undue assumptions about the background of the readers. This attention to the needs of a disparate audience arose naturally from the fact that nearly all the chapters were originally written for the 1994 annual conference of the British Educational Research Association (BERA); so they were intended for the variety of people that might be expected there.

In organising the symposium on 'Race and Culture' at the 1994 annual BERA conference in Oxford, we had clear criteria guiding our choice of contributors and we used these criteria to guide who we approached to add the remaining chapters. Two of these criteria were central. First, we wanted to include researchers relatively new on the scene. Most of the writers are near, or at, the end of completing a PhD. Most of them have not published much before (though some have, and some of them are now publishing a number of papers, even books, from their doctoral research.) Secondly, the authors and their projects were chosen to represent a range of interests and perspectives in relation both to their own subject positions and to their research focus.

These criteria are rooted in methodological/epistemological principles. These include the importance of seeking out new perspectives (even if we do not share them) and also of making sure that we are familiar with research carried out by researchers who vary in their own subject position, for instance in relation to 'race' and gender. We also take the view that it is important to pay attention to all sectors of education from infant schools to higher education.

The contributors include writers of African-Caribbean, South Asian, and White ethnic backgrounds; both men and women. Some of them conducted research in collaboration with people from their own communities. Others researched questions which are at issue as a result of racisms in the community at large (including structural, institutional and personal racisms), but which could only be answered using evidence gathered with the co-operation of people from a range of ethnic communities. It must be noted that precisely who is included in one's 'own' community is not at all obvious. Indeed, although we have used the term 'community' in this paragraph, for all the contributors, including ourselves, the complexities of the term 'community' is always at issue. Certainly this complexity — and how to deal with it — is central to all the various new perspectives proposed in their chapters.

Just as the term 'community' is at issue, so are the terms 'race', 'racism' and 'antiracism'. This is apparent throughout the book, in all the chapters. Many of the contributors note the complexities and problems surrounding these terms. These complexities and problems have proved impossible to resolve in simple terms. As Fazal Rizvi has noted in his discussion of the term 'racism', the protean form which it assumes means that it is not possible to reach an 'agreed meaning with which to identify its salience' (Rizvi, 1993, p.1). Indeed we share the view of other theorists that agreement is not even a desirable goal. In this respect, we are following the arguments of writers like Stuart Hall who has long argued against 'extrapolating a common and universal structure to racism, which remains essentially the same, outside of its specific historical location' (1980, p.377).

We are sympathetic with those sharing this perspective (e.g. CCCS, 1982; Gilroy, 1990, Solomos and Back, 1994) who have abandoned the term 'racism' as a conceptual tool because they reckon it lacks discriminatory power. They claim that the term, 'racism', cannot hope to secure a firm analytical purchase on the range of different modalities it is meant to describe in different historical and political circumstances. A further reason for treating the term with caution is the emotional, moral and political connotations which it carries, as a result of its history as central to many 20th Century political struggles: over fascism, Nazism, colonialism, nationalism, neo- and post-colonialism, Black liberation and British party politics. This makes the use of analytical distinctions in influencing practical situations even more problematic. Nevertheless, however protean, a general term is still needed to point out the general direction of injustices rooted in a wide range of racisms. The argument here is that the term should never be taken at face value, as an analytical tool, as if it had a clear and agreed set of meanings.

If the status of 'racism' as an analytical tool is under fire, where does that leave its close relative, 'antiracism'? Since the late 1980s in Britain, 'antiracism' has suffered a crisis in confidence, brought about by criticisms both from those sympathetic to racial justice and from those antagonistic to it.

To begin with, the 1980s witnessed the persistent and invidious demonisation of antiracist education, as part of a more general attack on equal opportunities issues in the media, and in other modes of political and public discourse. Troyna and Carrington (1990) and Troyna (1993) show how far this campaign was orchestrated by the Conservative party in association with its various 'think tanks'. One of its main targets was local government. In this attack, the Conservative administrations between 1979 and 1987 focused attention on the alleged profligacy of Labour-controlled local authorities, and on their apparent determination to give greater priority to antiracism and related egalitarian initiatives than to the needs of the White (male, heterosexual, able-bodied) electorate. At that time, the outer London boroughs of Brent and Haringey and the soon-to-be-dissolved Inner London Education Authority loomed large in the demonology of Conservative political rhetoric. Richardson (1992) gives details of the media orchestration of Conservative attacks on Brent's Development Programme for Race Equality. This was a successful campaign. We note that 'loony left' has entered the language, as 'loony right' has not, in spite of the fact that right wing politics and its excesses were extremely unpopular, as opinion polls showed at the time.

Since 1987, a series of legislative measures have been introduced which were designed to bring fundamental, irreversible changes to the ways in which education has been organised, administered and funded since 1944. Above all, there has been a weakening of the part played by Local Education Authorities, and a tightening of control by central government over the expenditure of schools. Since the 1988 Education Reform Act, central government has taken a much greater role in setting the educational agenda. They have done this partly by holding the purse strings, and partly by building on the earlier campaigns to demonise programmes for social justice in order to deploy what Kate Myers (1990) calls 'equiphobia': 'hatred and fear of anything to do with equal opportunities in education'. It has been a remarkably successful tactic and it has become difficult for those advocating a policy for equality to 'speak its name'.

The strategy has been effective in terms of practical outcomes. Rosemary Deem and her colleagues (1992) have demonstrated the absence of awareness of social justice issues, especially those to do with 'race', in school governing bodies. Deem and her colleagues point out that governors:

> do not need to concern themselves with social justice in education. The principle of social justice is no part of the rhetoric of the 1980s reform legislation; indeed it is considered to be undesirable as an educational principle. (1992, p.220)

They go on to investigate how far governors in their ten case-study schools show a concern with 'equal opportunities', and found that, in line with a previous, more extensive, study, 'no governor expressed a wish to have any training in equal opportunities issues' (1992, p.221), though they were keen to receive training on budget management and legal responsibilities. Indeed social justice was not much evident in the course of governors' meetings, either as an issue, or, more disturbingly, as a practice. In particular, they found that 'racism is a feature of many meetings' (1992, p.222).

Section 11 is another example. Since 1990, Local Authorities have had to bid competitively for Section 11 funding, specifying ways in which projects meet specific criteria, including language skills and home-school links but *not* including the maintenance of cultural traditions among ethnic minority communities. The bidding process has been time-consuming and uncertain. Since April 1994, funding for Section 11 projects has been further threatened by new financial arrangements. It was decided that money available for education would no longer be ring-fenced by the Home Office. Resources have been transferred to the Single Regeneration Budget for promoting urban renewal, so that education projects now have to bid competitively against projects which might include housing, safety, rubbish collection and large construction projects (Wallace and McMahon, 1994; *TES* 9/9/94; *TES* 14/10/94; *Asian Times*, 3/12/94).

There are plenty of other areas suffering from this effective combination of central financial control and the deployment of equiphobia. Even where there is no systematic research or newspaper reporting, it is easy for anyone involved in education to see how little the educational agenda is driven by considerations of racial justice. To take one example, there is the demise of inservice education related to racial equality; to take another, there appears to be institutional paralysis at all levels in the face of evidence of the disproportionate exclusion of African-Caribbean boys.

While the story is not cheerful, it is possible to argue that the concerted attack has at least had the good effect of concentrating the minds of all those researchers and practitioners who are concerned with racial justice. It is now possible to discern a wide-spread realisation of the need to move beyond the polarities and mutual attacks which characterised the various antiracist factions of the eighties. For all the arguments and counter-arguments surrounding what Gilroy (1990) called 'The End of Anti-Racism' — and they are vigorous (Rattansi, 1992; Troyna, 1993a) — there appears to be a new willingness to resolve these differences by giving serious consideration to new approaches. Indeed this book, itself, is an example of such a willingness. Certainly the two editors would not reach agreement about these questions of 'antiracism', but we had no difficulty co-operating on this project to further it. Indeed, we would like to emphasise that an important purpose of the book is the questioning and re-drawing of mainstream categories and boundary lines in the area of racisms and antiracism.

The book as a whole should be seen as contributing to the project of providing information and theoretical perspectives for the educational debate which still influences the practice of teachers and other educationists with respect to the issues of 'race' (in spite of the best efforts of the Right). It aims to re-define and re-align current polarised positions. It is to this end that it presents a range of new research rooted in this context of re-thinking the theoretical frameworks for research into antiracism, culture and social justice. There is, of course, no consensus among the contributors, any more than between the editors. However, there are some emerging patterns in the kinds of theoretical frameworks found helpful.

We would like to comment on the wide range of theoretical frameworks that are used in this collection. They are drawn from feminism, European Theory, Black studies, Black feminism, and cultural studies — some of them from postmodernist or post-structuralist perspectives. It is also notable how far the frameworks have gone beyond mere criticism of add-on or hierarchical models of oppression. That is, they escape the trap of focusing only on racial categories, to the exclusion of other structural sources of oppression: Black and White femininities and masculinities are in question, as are issues of social class. It is striking how far the research methods and the analysis of the data generated are irretrievably rooted in issues related to both social class and gender, as well as in racial issues, rather than in just one of these frames.

For instance, the research frameworks used by Neal, Reed and Reay mean that their data could not be analysed only with respect to antiracism without considerable distortion. The analysis in the chapter by Bhatti depends on attention to both class and gender, even though at first glance the focus on Asian children might be expected to confine attention to racial issues only. Further, the narrowness of research predicated on 'male-as-norm', or 'middle-class-as-norm' is avoided. For instance, it is notable that both Connolly and Sewell give a gender-sensitive analysis, although they are males researching males.

A particular strength of the contributions is that they not only display considerable theoretical sophistication and innovation but also all are rooted in empirical data recently collected. In this they go beyond much other recent work which all too often takes up only a theoretical perspective, unmodified by encounters with actual children and schools, or, on the other hand, merely collects items of data which mean little since they are so little analysed. The trouble is, no doubt, that under-funding in institutions of Higher Education for research on race, means that expensive data are hard to come by. The gap has been filled by so-called 'grey research' — statistics on 'race' collected by LEAs and central government, with a minimum of analysis or theoretical sophistication. As we commented, local government has been left with very few resources to pay for expensive theoretical analysis.

In this book, by contrast, the new theoretical perspectives and the new data are not separate issues. The data, and the methods of collecting them, are understood and evaluated within the assorted methodologies, epistemologies and ethical principles of the contributors.

Organisation and content of the book

Looking at the collection as a whole, some significant themes appear. Most importantly, there is the attention to social justice as a whole, as we have already pointed out. There are other significant themes. They include: the importance of silences (Neal, Bhatti, Reay, Williams, Mirza) and the impact of insult (Hatcher, Connolly); the significance of the process of discourse, as rooted in material conditions, but not determined by them (Sewell, Haw, Hatcher, Reay, Connolly); and the recognition of the irreducible complexity of the situation leading to complex, multiple, flexible resolutions: no quick fixes or once-for-always solutions. This last point is something which is brought out strongly by all the writers.

With so many overlapping continuities and interlocking themes, we decided to order the chapters in terms of the order of age-range studied; that is, from Higher Education, (Neal) through to pre-school/infant (Williams). The book ends with data on the research process itself: a critical look at the dynamics of carrying out antiracist, feminist research, and the complexities of retaining a hold on the political project while addressing specific positioning of both researchers and their 'subjects'.

In 'A Question of Silence?', Neal draws on ethnographic field work to examine equal opportunities policies and antiracist initiatives in two institutions of Higher Education. She examines the issues of ownership of the equal opportunities policies; at the marginalisation of the structures created to implement them; and at the development of hierarchies within the areas of equal opportunities discourses.

Moving on to secondary education, Sewell focuses on African-Caribbean boys, Haw on Muslim girls, Bhatti on Asian children and Raphael Reed on secondary school teachers. Sewell addresses the issue of recent Black male youth culture and its role in explaining the performance of Black males in school. In 'A Phallic Response to Schooling', evidence is drawn from a study of African-Caribbean boys in a city secondary school, using their (particular) perceptions of Black youth culture. Haw examines how the discourses of gender and 'race' are articulated in the educational experiences of Muslim girls. In 'Why Muslim Girls are More Feminist in Muslim Schools', she draws on research in a private Muslim girls' school and a single sex state school with a high proportion of Muslim girls. In 'A Journey into the Unknown', Bhatti explores the different perspectives of Asian children, and their parents and teachers on their schooling. She uses data collected in an extensive ethnographic study of a school and the parents of its Asian pupils, to examine the complex and fragmented data arising from the very different sets of informants. Raphael Reed uses data from a research project based on life-histories to examine how teachers who have sustained their radical commitment since the 1980s have responded to a policy context which materially repositions and ideologically deconstructs the more radical discourses of 'equal opportunities' in education. In 'Reconceptualising Equal Opportunities in the 1990s' she identifies some recurring themes in the various individual voices she reports.

The primary phase of education provides the context for the next four chapters, by Hatcher, Reay, Connolly and Williams. Hatcher addresses the topic of 'race' within the cultures of White children. In 'Racism and Children's Cultures', he draws on research into children aged mainly 10 and 11 years old in three predominantly White primary schools. The research examines how racist insults are used as interaction strategies and analyses some of the complexities of the relationship such strategies bear to the attitudes of children. In 'Using Habitus to Look at 'Race' and Class in Children's Peer Group Cultures', Reay uses evidence from participant observation in two urban primary school classrooms. She uses Bourdieu's concept of habitus to focus on the ways in which attitudes of cultural superiority and inferiority are ingrained in daily interactions, in particular those of White, middle class people. The focus is less on racial insult and more on silences. Connolly investigates the effects of policies intended to deal with the effects of racisms in primary schools. In 'Reconsidering Multicultural/antiracist Strategies in Education', he uses data from a year-long ethnographic study in the school. He uses a context-specific analysis to show the unexpected effects of a strategy of promoting football, targeted at Black boys. Williams' chapter moves the focus outside the school to the parents of African-Caribbean children. In 'How Black Children Might Survive Education', she reports a preliminary investigation into ways in which African-Caribbean parents can prepare their children for school. Drawing on responses to questionnaires and interviews, she explores the possibilities open to Black mothers who have to support their children in schools.

Finally, in 'Some Ethical Dilemmas in Fieldwork', Mehreen Mirza examines the ethical dilemmas of researching gender/'race' issues. Drawing on the author's own research, as a South Asian woman, into the educational experiences of South Asian women and girls, it questions current, standard, feminist and antiracist approaches to resolving the ethical and practical dilemmas of research.

Chapter 1

A question of silence?
Antiracist discourses and initiatives in Higher Education: Two case studies

Sarah Neal

Introduction — setting the scene

In November 1994 *The Times* newspaper carried a small report, but on the front page, on the findings of a student union survey conducted at Oxford University, which found that four in five women students had experienced some form of sexual harassment. Although these are shocking figures in themselves, the survey found that even more prevalent was the experience of racial harassment. Ninety seven percent of Black and other minority ethnic[1] students reported having experienced verbal abuse or physical attack (*The Times*, 8.11.94).

In 1988 the Commission for Racial Equality (CRE) exposed the racist exclusion admissions practices of St. George's Medical School, part of the University of London, whereby Black and other minority ethnic students were systematically being denied student places in the School (CRE, 1988). The Oxford survey and the CRE investigation have both provided rare public glimpses into the extent of racism in Higher Education.

Unlike pre-sixteen education, Higher Education, with its tradition of studying 'those out there', has rarely itself been the subject of social research, especially in relation to race (and gender). It is as if 'racial discrimination is something to be studied in the world beyond the campus; it is rarely regarded as a real world issue within [the institution]' (*Times Higher Educational Supplement*, 1983, quoted in Williams et al, 1989, p.8). Yet Higher Education presents an ideal research site, for a number of reasons. It is a social institution which is characterised by contradiction: on the one hand it has traditional humanitarian and liberal associations — even, due mainly to a brief period in the late 1960s and early 1970s, radical associations. New middle class theorists (Parkin, 1968; Gouldner, 1979; Offe, 1984) have identified Higher Education as a crucial site for the politicisation of 'welfare professionals'. Yet on the other hand, Higher Education is intensely hierarchical and individualistic; it has mainly serviced a privileged minority and has had a functional role in furnishing the class and knowledge needs of the state in capitalist society (Halsey, 1992). In the latter this can be seen nowhere more clearly than in the area of race (Gilroy, 1980; Bourne, 1982, Lawrence, 1982, Carby 1982). As Goldberg argues:

> knowledge production, in general and in the social sciences especially, has ... done much at various watershed moments to create, authorise, legitimate and license the figures of racial otherness, the fabrication of racial selves and social subjects (1992, p.208).

This chapter centrally posits that Higher Education has now to be viewed as the social institution that it has always been. The post-Robbins era and, somewhat ironically, Conservative Higher Education policy (massification, the post-binary system, the Further and Higher Education Act, 1992) have succeeded in prising Higher Education from its seemingly remote location at the privileged peripheries of society and reset it more centrally. The late 1980s and early 1990s have witnessed the cautious arrival of equal opportunities discourses and policies onto the Higher Education agenda (see, for example, the CVCP *Guidelines on Equal Opportunities*

2

in Universities, 1991) and this can be understood, to some extent, as a reflection of this relocation.

While I have explored equal opportunities discourses and policies in Higher Education elsewhere (see Neal, 1996), what remains acutely under-investigated, and in sharp contrast to pre-sixteen education (Gillborn, 1990; Troyna and Hatcher, 1992; Troyna, 1993a; Mirza, 1992) is race and antiracist discourses and initiatives in Higher Education.

The existing literature concerned with Higher Education and equal opportunities policies is limited and has had as its focus equal opportunities rather than antiracism. Until very recently (apart from Cockburn's (1988) qualitatively based, internal report on women's equality for the then Lancashire Polytechnic) the Higher Education and equal opportunities literature has been quantitatively based. The CRE funded *Words or Deeds: a review of equal opportunity policies in Higher Education* (Williams et al, 1989) provides, via questionnaire returns, a valuable national overview of equality policies in sixty-eight Higher Education institutions. The work of Mason et al into equal opportunities references and visual representations of Black and other minority ethnic staff and students in 'old' university (1990) and 'new' university prospectuses (1993) again offers a valuable and innovative glimpse into one aspect of equal opportunities in Higher Education. More closely related to my own research has been the just completed research of Weiner et al (1995) which examined, through three case studies, equitable staffing policies in higher and further education. This chapter is an attempt to move beyond some of the limitations of the existing literature. Perhaps the most obvious of these has been both the tendency to accept equal opportunities as a 'given good' and the paucity of a specific focus on antiracism. Although this body of literature does incorporate a race dimension, this has been collapsed into a broader equal opportunities framework of racial equality rather than any focus on antiracism as an anti-oppressive concept and series of strategic initiatives.

As Higher Education has to be understood as a social institution, then equal opportunities, in the classical liberal interpretation at least, has to be understood as a form of *social policy*. It has become the main, or the acceptable, strategy used by the state and other institutions/organisations for countering discrimination and disadvantage. Yet antiracism has never acquired any such acceptability. Since its Labour town hall heyday in the

3

mid-1980s, antiracism has become a battered and damaged concept, receiving such a sustained attack from by the right and the media that this became known as anti-antiracism (Solomos, 1989; 1993). During the 1990s antiracism has also received sustained criticism from some commentators on the left (Gilroy, 1987; 1990; Macdonald et al, 1989; Modood, 1992) who have condemned the moral and municipal antiracism of the 1980s for its reification of 'race' and the reliance of antiracism on the threadbare Black/White dichotomy. However the criticisms of the left, severe though they have been, have always stopped just short of an outright condemnation of antiracism and seek to offer instead a revised (more sophisticated) approach to antiracist thinking and strategies.[2] There is an element in this situation of being caught between 'a rock and a hard place' which has been expressed by Gilroy when he notes that antiracism 'has become impossible to utter in the still places where ... formal processes operate but in view of the jeopardy in which Black people live then its use remains imperative' (1992, xi).

Focus

At its broadest level this chapter seeks to examine how antiracism, as a discourse and as a strategy, has appeared, *if at all*, within the context of Higher Education. To do this it draws on two Higher Education institution case studies — both 'new' universities — which presented the core field work of my ethnographic doctoral research project.[3] The chapter will initially examine the equal opportunities policy texts which were made available to me in each case study. My concern here is to explore the silences of these texts in relation to antiracism; in other words to look at what the texts did not say and what they obscured rather than at what they did actually say. The main part of the chapter then uses my interview data to explore the various ways in which race, racial equality and antiracism were actually discussed by the research respondents.

Both the 'new' university case studies, Northfield University and Castlebrook University, had rapidly expanded during the late 1980s and early 1990s. Northfield University, situated in a relatively small, prosperous town in northern England, had an extensive and innovative equal opportunities structure (it uses Section 11 money to fund a number of race equality initiatives) and a known commitment to equality issues. Castlebrook University is located in one of the poorer inner London boroughs and although it has, to some extent, a public equal opportunities face, this is due mainly to it formerly being under ILEA control — its present equal opportunities structure is minimal.

Although documentation has comprised an important element of the research data, the primary source of material has come through semi-structured interviewing of three target groups: members of senior management teams; members of staff with a formal responsibility for equal opportunities and members of staff who were informally involved with, or interested in, equality issues.

The research has had an upwards gaze. In other words, the site of inquiry has been institutions and the activities of, often powerful, professionals. From its conception I have approached the research from feminist and antiracist perspectives. By this I mean that I have problematised race (and gender) in the specific fields of discourse within the research (Connolly, 1993; Back and Solomos, 1992; Troyna, 1993a;b; see also Neal 1995 for a discussion of the political and ethical dilemmas experienced conducting this type of research).

The policy texts

It is not my intention extensively to rehearse the content and nature of the case studies' equal opportunities policy texts here. What I want to emphasise is the *standardisation* in the content and style of the policy texts and their adherence to a liberal or 'fair chance/removal of barriers' equal opportunities model.

Although the equal opportunities documentation may have differed in quantity between the case studies, there was a high degree of similarity in that which did exist in terms of the areas covered and the style in which they were written. For example, the equal opportunities statement of intent, perhaps the most widely disseminated aspect of an institution's equal opportunities policy, were almost identical in the two case studies, containing predictable anti-discriminatory intentions. Similarly, documents covering equal opportunities in academic affairs (staff — fair interviewing; students — access; curriculum — multicultural/gender sensitive) were again produced according to a standardised or prescribed formula. The third central policy area common to both the case studies was their sexual and racial harassment codes of practice. These, too, read as if they had been written as variations on the same model. The structural spin-offs of these policies — monitoring programmes, equal opportunities committees, advisors, units — reflect the same *rationalist* and *technicist* approaches as those within the policy documents (Ball, 1994). There were few indications of more imaginative or creative approaches to equality issues. My own research, which could have represented such an approach for the institutions, was never treated as such. Although I had assured each institution at the outset of the research, that I would be willing to disseminate it, no path was ever beaten impatiently (or otherwise) to my door to elicit the nature of my findings.

Probing silence: getting behind the policy texts

I treated the policy texts with caution. Organisational policy texts serve a variety of purposes and cannot simply be read at face value. I expected to find a discrepancy between operational and presentational data. Van Manen (1981) has described presentational data as:

> those appearances that informants strive to maintain in the eyes of ... outsiders ... Data in this category deals [sic] far more with the manufacturer's image of idealised doings than with the on-going practical activities actually engaged in by members of the group (quoted in Loveland, 1988, p.206).

However, what was significant for me in my analysis of the case studies' policy texts was not simply the discrepancies between their claims and the everyday reality of the institution but the omission in itself of any references specifically to antiracism. Where 'race' was alluded to or mentioned, it was done in terms of strategies for *racial equality* and never in terms of *antiracist* strategies.

A prevailing feature which characterised the case studies' equal opportunities policy texts was their extensive and shared use of 'condensation symbols' (Edelman, 1964), 'slogan systems' (Apple, 1977) or 'essentially contested concepts' (Gallie, 1956). Condensation symbols refer to terms or phrases that contain a particular emotional impact and positive associations while at the same time retaining an elasticity which means that they are open to different and often competing interpretations. Most obvious is the term 'equal opportunities' itself, but such terms as 'access', 'multiculturalism', 'equality' can also be understood as condensation symbols. The discourses associated with these phrases often conceal conflicting ideologies and a diversity of interests for those involved in policy making processes and implementation.

While Troyna and Williams (1986) have argued that the deployment of condensation symbols in the part of policy makers is deliberate, Edelman (1977, p.20) states that 'there is no implication that elites consciously mould political myths and rituals to serve their own ends', but that they are created by 'living within the social texture'. I would posit that there is a mixture of both: that to a certain extent, there is a deliberate deployment of condensation symbols or slogan systems but that, by their very nature, these take on their own varied connotations. However, it is clear that condensation symbols are able to hide gaps and ambiguities within policy statements. Within this context I want to argue that the absence of the concept or phrase 'antiracism' in the policy texts has to be attributed to the severe limitations that 'antiracism' has as a condensation symbol. Unlike 'equal opportunities', it lacks the necessary degree of vagueness and its connotations are not unequivocally positive, i.e. its usage does not widely provoke the ideas of harmony, consensus or joint endeavour.

Even though it was absent from the policy texts, I asked each respondent in the interviews what they took antiracism to mean and whether they saw antiracism as a separate issue or inclusive to the broader equal opportunities paradigm. Perhaps not surprisingly, this was widely perceived as a difficult or (significantly) puzzling question. Overwhelmingly, antiracism was defined as meaning 'not discriminating against Black people'. Although Gilroy (1990, p.207) has warned that 'we should be wary of collapsing anti-racism, let alone Black emancipation, into equal opportunities', the majority of respondents located antiracism firmly within the terrain of equal opportunities and it was not seen as being, or needing to be, a separate strategy.

There was some evidence in the interviews that the high profile anti-antiracism attacks from the right and the press during the 1980s had had some impact on Higher Education — antiracism was negatively associated with political municipal campaigns — and this fed into an institutional avoidance of the pursuit of specifically antiracist policies:

> I'm not in favour of separating out policies for Black students and
> staff. I'm very critical of organisations that have done that in the past
> ... like ILEA and some of the other London boroughs ... All equal

7

opportunities aspects are as important as the others (Head of Human Resources, Castlebrook University).

The paucity in references to antiracism in the policy texts and its collapse into equal opportunities in the interviews is a reflection of the problematic status of antiracism within Higher Education's equality discourses.

A feature common to both case studies was the senior management ownership of equal opportunities policies. Northfield and Castlebrook had Equal Opportunities Committees which were chaired by senior management representatives, usually the Vice-Chancellor or the Director. In Castlebrook University, management ownership of the equality policies was heavily pronounced. The University's Equal Opportunities Committee was almost completely made up of (unelected) senior management figures, with only one place given over to a staff representative. Apart from a Disability Unit and Equal Opportunities Committee, the University had no other equal opportunities structure. Similarly in Northfield University its commitment to equal opportunities policies was widely associated with the personal commitment of the University's Director. The narrow senior management ownership of equality policies had resulted in the somewhat ironic situation of equality issues being a senior management concern. The corollary of this process has been that equality policy process are very much under management control — as this excerpt from my interview with the Director of Northfield University illustrates:

SN: What do you see as the role of the senior management team in relation to equal opportunities in the University?

Director: We have an Equal Opportunities Committee that *I chair* and this is technically a committee which is *advisory to me* and it's the vehicle by which our major policy initiatives and procedures are discussed ... and taken *via myself*, to the appropriate bodies like the University Board or the Academic Board ... *so I see myself as having the responsibility for taking those issues forward* (my emphasis).

The perception of the role of senior management displayed here clearly involves elements of control and veto. The role of senior management does present a dilemma in relation to equality policy processes. In the case

8

studies the chairing of their equal opportunities committees by senior management can be seen as an important feature in adding weight to those committees. Yet a too heavy top-down model (without a consultative process) has a direct impact both on the ownership of the equality policies and on what becomes a policy or what reaches the equality policy agenda. It is within this context that the absence of antiracism as a policy approach or as concept, has to be understood. I noted earlier that the equal opportunities policies in the case studies adhered closely to a liberal 'removal of barriers' model (Jewson and Mason, 1986) and that the acceptability of equal opportunities discourses within Higher Education relates closely to their vagueness and elasticity of interpretation. In the current 'equiphobic' climate (Myers, 1990), when the accusation of 'political correctness' is almost more terrifying to institutions than accusations of racism (or sexism), antiracism has an increasing paucity in terms of offering any seductive qualities.

Questioning silence

Using micro-political perspectives

Looking behind the policy texts, what became apparent was the messy, contested and fractured 'everyday-world' of the case studies. While organisation theorists have concentrated on structure and consensus in educational organisations (see Handy and Aitken 1986), this focus has been criticised by some commentators (Ball, 1987; Blase, 1991; Weiner, 1992; Ball, 1994) who have posited that organisational theorists have been overly concerned with the role of rationalist and efficiency discourses in organisations and have consequently obscured the fact that organisations are sites of conflict, goal diversity, tension and domination which are bound together through micro-politics. As Blase (1991) has argued:

> Political theorists have argued that rational and systems models of organisations have failed to account for complexity, instability and conflict in organisational settings. They contend that such models also ignore individual differences, for example, in values, ideologies, choices, goals, interests, expertise, history, motivation and interpretation — factors central to the micropolitical perspective (p.3).

9

Elsewhere (Neal, 1996) I have drawn on micro-political perspectives to posit that the equal opportunities policies in the case studies were characterised by ideological disputation, goal diversity, conflict and power divisions (Ball, 1987, p.8). Taking these same perspectives, this chapter uses them as the framework in which I explored the ways in which race appeared in the specific fields of discourse in the research.

Hierarchies within the equal opportunities paradigm

Equal opportunities is an all-embracing paradigm. It evokes demands from a wide range of powerless groups[4]: what Anthias and Yuval-Davis (1992) have termed the 'equal opportunities community'. Yet equal opportunities policies have adopted a very sectionalist approach to the 'equal opportunities community'. Although powerless people are not simply Black or female or disabled or lesbian/gay or working class but almost inevitably form different combinations of these categories, the sectionalism of equal opportunities policies (and related resources) have served to produce a situation in which the various (sectionalised) categories of the equal opportunities community are forced into competing against each other for resources, financial and otherwise, so fracturing and dividing what may have been common interests. Anthias and Yuval-Davis describe an incident at the Greater London Council (GLC) in which they observed a bitter conflict between the Race Unit and the Women's Unit over who was to have prior claim to a newly appointed Black woman worker (1992, p.172). Ouseley (1990) has similarly commented on the competitive process in what he terms the 'bandwagon effect' of equal opportunity policies. Ouseley argues that race equality initiatives produced a wide by-product of benefits for and demands from other groups traditionally denied access to resources:

> Whenever anti-racism is used as a process for change in any institution it becomes a challenge to all unfair policies, practises and procedures, that ultimately leads to a clean up of the whole discriminatory apparatus of the local state or the institution under scrutiny (1990, p.142-3).

Since Anthias and Yuval-Davis and Ouseley were writing about the hierarchies that develop within equal opportunities in local authority settings, I was expecting similar patterns but with possible slight differences because the acute competition between oppressed groups over resources did not exist in the same forms and because of the top-down nature of the equal opportunities models in the case studies. So there was very little organised or sustained grass-roots-based equality activity. Consequently, I was interested in looking at how equal opportunities policies fragmented and why they tended to fragment in the ways that they did. In other words, I was exploring hierarchy in terms of what was 'comfortable' within equal opportunities discourses (reflected in a greater degree of policies/resources/attention) and what was 'uncomfortable' (reflected in fewer policies/resources/attention) and why.

Most obviously, a hierarchy had developed within equal opportunities in the form of more policies and procedures relating to gender. Gender was also the issue which most respondents felt comfortable discussing and this cut across all the case studies. There was a close correlation between the ways in which equal opportunities activity tended to fragment around particular issues and what areas of equal opportunities were seen as being more 'comfortable'. Gender then, had a secure place at the top of the hierarchy — gender had been on the equality agenda for the longest period and this had produced an established policy focus on such traditional issues as maternity provision, job-share schemes, flexi-time, child care provision, better lighting on campus and sexual harassment. There was a familiarity about these issues, and the institutions studied demonstrated a willingness to develop policy responses to them. However, I would argue that this willingness was underpinned by the nature of these issues, that they can be understood as relating to traditional areas of women's lives, i.e. their domestic roles and their need for protection from ('outside'/'stranger') sexual violence. In the two case studies, sexual (and to some extent, racial) harassment policies were the most contested area of the equality policies. Their contentiousness has to be placed in the context that sexual and racial harassment policies represent the 'penal code' of equal opportunities. Sexual harassment policies are designed to address the behaviour and attitudes of 'known men' i.e male members of university staff.

Gender, then, was an acceptable aspect of equal opportunities, as long as it could be approached through non-threatening policies. Positive action was also acceptable, as it reinforced the domestic divisions of labour and women's vulnerability to 'outside'/'stranger' sexual violence.

ANTIRACISM, CULTURE AND SOCIAL JUSTICE IN EDUCATION

Hostility to or doubts about the necessity of sexual harassment codes and the absence of positive action policies to aid increases in women's presence in positions of power, either in senior management teams or academic hierarchies, is a reflection of this attitude.

Also maintaining the comfortableness of gender was the projection of gender as *White*. In the policy texts and the interviews there was rarely any recognition of gender being a disparate and fractured category. Many of those who were in positions of having a formal responsibility for equal opportunities implementation were women, women who, almost invariably, explained their commitment to equal opportunities in terms of having a primary interest in gender, without relating gender to other forms of oppression or its racialisation. For example the Co-ordinator of the Women's Unit in Northfield University admitted that, although she would like to see it, there was actually no liaison between the Unit and the University's Race Equality Centre. The paucity in identification of an interface between race and gender in the policy documents, and by the majority of the equal opportunity 'workers', meant that Black and other minority ethnic women had been effectively made invisible. When I questioned the whiteness of gender in the interviews, it was not rare for very stereotypical stereotypes of Black and other minority ethnic women to emerge:

Many of the Afro-Caribbean women students here often have dependent children and they might be single parents, so part of our equal opportunities policy is to have good child care provisions and have things like courses not starting at nine in the morning every day (Head of Human Resources, Castlebrook University).

Perhaps one of the most shocking responses came from the University Secretary in Northfield University, who told me that she had been involved in various outreach projects which were trying to encourage more Black/Asian women from the local community to enrol on courses:

Of course we've tried to get women from the Asian population to come in and do part-time study but the culture is that they are not let out if you like ... their husbands and families don't let them out and have very strict rules about their freedom ... in some racial groups women are treated in a really, really oppressed way, you know, to the point of arranged marriages and having to sit at the back of the

12

synagogue or whatever it is ... They are not treated in ... with the same kind of freedoms.

Where Black women were visible through their actual presence on the (academic) staff in an institution, they were cast in the role of 'super-women' — Black women who had reached their position against all odds and were consequently viewed as 'race experts'. At Northfield University, a Black woman lecturer explained how she felt she was treated like 'some kind of rare, exotic creature who did, quotes 'race work', and who it was best not to get to close to'.

So although gender can be seen as a comfortable or acceptable area of the equal opportunities paradigm, this was subject to certain conditions — that gender equality policies related to traditional areas of women's lives, that women's needs were homogeneous and that gender could be defined in terms of the experience of White women.

Alongside gender, disability was an area that was rapidly climbing the equal opportunities hierarchy. Disability was increasingly gaining a policy and resource focus and, again, represented an area that respondents identified as 'easier' to work around:

> People are generally happy to talk about disability, although if there is actually a person with disabilities in the same room then there is often a lot of embarrassment (Lecturer, Castlebrook University).

Castlebrook University had recently created both a Disability Committee and a Disability Unit, yet had no committees for gender or 'race'. The University had a separate policy document relating to disability, whereas gender, 'race' and sexuality were dealt with together in the same policy documents.

As was the case for gender, the willingness of an institution to address a disabilities agenda had to be placed in the context of that agenda's ability to reinforce certain conceptions about the nature of disability — dependency — and the needs of people with disabilities being overwhelmingly physical. That 'embarrassment' emerges when people with disabilities themselves become involved in the policy processes, indicates that there are far more complex (political) issues that surround disability (see Morris, 1989). However such issues are submerged under policy processes that centre on concerns about the provision of lifts, ramps, widened doorways, hearing loops, health and safety etc. For example, although

Castlebrook University's disability policy document stated in its introduction that the university regards disability as integral area of equal opportunities, the remainder of the document is given over to information on the geographical accessability of the University to students and staff with disabilities.

I am not arguing against the provision of an accessible learning/teaching environment, but rather against the way that concerns with this take place outside of any wider context of thinking about disability and ableism. It is for this reason that disability has become an acceptable or easy area within equal opportunities policy making.

The equal opportunities community became hierarchically fractured according to the ability of the institution to *depoliticise* the categories and related issues. In other words, policy initiatives around both gender and disability could be reduced to fit most neatly into the classical liberalism of a 'removal of barriers' model of equal opportunities, while 'race' and sexuality represent more troublesome and less reductionist categories. Sexuality had a minimalist presence in the policy documents, tending not to appear beyond a mention in the lists of groups against whom discriminatory behaviour was unacceptable. If it was referred to in interviews, it was identified as a 'difficult' area. Not surprisingly, sexuality was the only area of equal opportunities in which no rhetorical claims were made along the lines of wanting to see fairer representations of lesbian and gay staff or students. In the case studies' equal opportunities programmes, sexuality was in effect a 'no-go' issue .

Breaking silence

Asking about 'race'

'Race' was the area most commonly identified as difficult and uncomfortable. Unlike gender or disability, 'race' is impossible to depoliticise, yet unlike sexuality, 'race' had a very central presence within equal opportunities policies. When I asked respondents why they thought gender had a higher profile than 'race', the simplistic and frequent reply was that this was because there were more women than Black people in the institution (and society) or else because gender had been around as an issue for longer. When I probed further and asked respondents why they saw 'race' as a more difficult issue than gender, three clearly identifiable themes

14

emerged in the responses, all of which tended to cast Black people and other minority ethnic people, rather than racism, as problematic. The first of these themes was represented in the argument that an institution has a responsibility to provide equality of opportunity (a 'level playing field') but that it could go no further than this, i.e. that it was then up to Black people. This line was most commonly associated with senior management responses:

> We make sure we've got good access routes, we can make sure that the curriculum reflects our multicultural society and we make sure that our racial harassment code is in order. We want to ensure that doors aren't closed for Black people but we can't bring about equality of outcome (Vice-Chancellor, Castlebrook University).

The second theme was represented in the 'race is a very complex area' argument. Despite the accuracy of this observation, when this argument surfaced from both senior management and the respondents with formal responsibility for equal opportunities, this complexity was often qualified in terms of the existence of a 'lot of racism' between Black people themselves:

> Actually the majority of racial problems that we have here tend not to be between White and Black people but between the different cultures ... those students who come from different African countries and between our Afro-Caribbean students and our Asian students ... and that's particularly difficult to deal with (Pro Vice-Chancellor, Castlebrook University).

This theme can be again be heard in the comments made by the Chair of the Race Advisory Group at Northfield University:

> There are such a wide range of issues associated with race ... There are inter-racial issues between Black and Asian populations ... It's such a multiple. With gender it's quite easy because you've just got male and female, but with race ... Gender can get people's backs up but with race ... well, it gets people's backs up too but it makes them feel uncomfortable as well.

This invoking of (natural) cultural hostilities not only draws on new racist discourses (Barker, 1981) and deflects attention away from institutional racism but, perhaps most importantly, it projects the idea that 'race' is impossible to understand and that it is difficult for White people to know what to do about it. Directly linked with this is the third theme I encountered widely: the 'fear' theme. By this I mean that there was a tendency for White respondents to present themselves as being unsure about how to talk about 'race' issues and about Black people:

> With gender, people are relatively happy about what the issues are and what needs to be done, but with race ... it's foggy ... It's not often talked about and people feel unsure about what they should be doing and what language to use — they don't want to look like idiots and they don't want to offend anyone (Co-ordinator, Women's Unit, Northfield University).

The idea that White people were frightened of 'race', of saying the 'wrong thing', of exposing themselves as racist, surfaced numerous times in the interviewing process. The sub-text of this seemed to be that Black people and antiracism had managed to create a code of cultural morality which White people had become terrified of transgressing. In my interview with the Chair of the Race Advisory Group (a White man and Dean of the Business Faculty), he recalled with emotion an incident in which he had been invited to speak at a forum for Black women in business:

> It was a *petrifying experience* and I made a complete fool of myself. There were Black women talking about their experiences and then when it was my turn to speak ... I was stupid to accept the invitation ... I introduced myself as a White man and that was a bad statement to make because it immediately discriminated against everyone else who was Black and female — so I'd exposed my own racism. It made me extremely uncomfortable. I couldn't excuse it, I had no other excuse than that I was *petrified* and I didn't know what to do. *I think that's what people feel when their racism is exposed* (My emphasis).

What is interesting in these situations was the role in which I was cast: as some form of 'expert' who, despite being White, knew, by virtue of the type of questions that I was asking, the 'right things to say'. At the end of the above interview the respondent asked me if I thought there were any aspects of the language he had used which I felt he should be thinking (critically) about.

Increasingly I came to see this presentation of 'fear' in relation to race in the interviews as a form of almost cathartic 'confessionalism'; in other words I represented a safe zone in which to make these admissions[5].

The concern with 'saying the right thing' actually served as a let-out clause for not saying the right thing, but, more fundamentally, it served to stop 'race' and racism being thought about in any real or meaningful way within the institutions and this was reflected in the limited amount of tangible commitment that had been given to tackling 'race' issues.

In the case studies the attempts to depoliticise 'race' and to box it into categories of access, multicultural curricula, monitoring and racial harassment codes had been only partially successful. My explorations into why (White) respondents found 'race' difficult and uncomfortable illustrated the extent to which 'race' had continued to seep out of such technicist and rationalist approaches and maintained a contested and political profile which bubbled just below the surfaces of the equality discourses within the universities.

Because of the need to contain and control the discourse in this position, 'race' had been exiled to the peripheries of the equal opportunities agenda. The clearest example of this was presented in Northfield University where, despite having quite extensive structures in place to address racial equality — the Section 11 funded initiatives (a Racial Equality Centre, significantly located with the University's Access Unit, and six individual posts that circulated departments) and the Race Advisory Committee, race remained at the bottom of the equal opportunities hierarchy. While this situation was acknowledged by senior management in the University, no responsibility was taken for it:

> Policy development [for race] has been far more difficult in this organisation and yet we've had special funding for the Racial Equality Centre ... *I don't know why it is*, all I know is that it's been more difficult to get policy development on race, always. Race policy has lagged behind gender policy and yet we have many more structures doing the work ... The issues are more difficult. I think you can treat gender issues in an homogeneous way; you can say all women experience similar kinds of discrimination but I don't think you can say the same is true with all the different racial groups (University Secretary, *my emphasis*).

A number of commentators (Solomos, 1983; Ben-Tovim et al, 1986; Ouseley, 1984, 1990; Anthias and Yuval-Davis, 1992) have argued that race equality initiatives and the structures put in place to implement them have a particular vulnerability to being pushed to the edges of an institution's activities and priorities, making them 'easy targets ... to isolate, thus reducing further their potential and scope for getting close enough to power structures to challenge them' (Ouseley, 1984, p.144). The same analysis can clearly be applied to my own research findings.

Conclusion

In this chapter I have sought to posit that although equal opportunities discourses and policies have obtained a place on Higher Education agenda, antiracism as a specific discourse and as a strategic approach has not. Antiracism, in either its traditional form or any revised form, has been avoided in policy formation and rejected as a conceptual framework for institutions to work within. I have argued that the willingness of the case studies to address an equal opportunities agenda has been dependent on an institution's ability to *de-politicise* equality issues and approach them through a rationalist and technicist policy framework. To some extent 'race' has been subjected to this same process: in the case studies 'race' had become reduced to the categories of access, multiculturalism, racial harassment codes and ethnic monitoring. These form *standardised* responses that can only have a minimalist impact on the Black experience of Higher Education or the racist processes of the everyday world of universities.

From this I conclude that the race equality initiatives and discourses that surround them in the case studies bear only a tangential relationship to the fundamental questions of antiracism in Higher Education (Ball, 1994). Antiracism is an oppositional discourse which is inevitably weighed down with an array of political baggage and it is because of its political profile and the implications of this profile that it has been avoided and shrouded in silence by Higher Education institutions.

Notes

1. I use the term/category 'Black' to refer to people of African Caribbean and South Asian decent. I use the term/category 'minority ethnic' to refer to those belonging to/identifying as another minority group. I recognise the limitations of these terms and do. not use them to negate difference or imply homogeneity or to deny that these are constructed definitions, as is the term 'White'.

2. The investigation into the murder of an Asian pupil by a White peer at a Manchester school (Macdonald et al, 1989) was critical of the school's antiracist policies and this was widely perceived by the right and the press as 'proof' of the dangers of antiracism. In response, Macdonald issued the following press statement:

    > It is because we consider the task of combating racism to be such a critical part of the function of schooling and education that we condemn symbolic, moral and doctrinaire anti-racism. We urge care, rigour and caution in the formulating and implementing of such policies because we consider the struggle against racism and racial injustice to an essential element in the struggle for social justice. (Reprinted in Macdonald et al 1989, xxiii-xxiv).

3. The research has been funded by the ESRC and supervised by Professor John Solomos.

4. While I. use the term 'powerless group', I recognise that the term has severe limitations both in its generic vagueness and in its inability to account for the complexities of overlap; i.e. powerless groups becoming powerful groups in shifting contexts.

5. Elsewhere I have discussed the implications and ethical dilemmas of White people interviewing White people about race and racism in the research process (Neal, 1995).

Chapter 2

A phallic response to schooling:
Black masculinity and race in an inner-city comprehensive

Tony Sewell

In his study of masculinities, Mac an Ghaill (1994) talks about how in ethnographic studies a certain incident captures the essence or kernel of your research. This happened to me when I showed a video of a programme by Lenny Henry. In the sketch Henry plays the feckless Delbert who makes his living by doing scams. I showed the video to a group of 15 year old African Caribbean students. One of the questions I asked them was whether there was any difference between the scams that White boys do compared to Blacks. There was a universal agreement that White boys would do only scams which were not blatant and less likely to get them caught. Ironically, they took pride in the more daring or up-front scams that they linked with themselves. When I asked if they thought that the White boys might be more clever with their sneaky scams, one boy replied: 'No way, sir, the White boys here are just 'pusses'. They haven't got the balls like a Black man. Most of them go on as if they are batty men (homosexual)'. There was a loud cheer in agreement.

It was then that I realised that something had gone seriously wrong in the way that these boys were conceptualising 'race', masculinity and schooling. This incident pointed to the need to explore more deeply the connection between the unstable categories of 'race' and masculinity in the context of school life.

This chapter explores the close relationship between racism and gender in the context of masculine identities in school. Mac an Ghaill (1994) has pointed to the complex inter-relationships between 'race' and sexuality for boys in multi-ethnic schools. He quotes Fanon's observation (1967 p.160):

> if one wants to understand the racial situation psychoanalytically ... as it is experienced by individual consciousness, considerable import-ance must be given to sexual phenomena.

As Hall (1988, p.29) has commented, it is impossible to understand contemporary racisms without ' crossing the questions of racism irrevoc-ably with the questions of sexuality.' In this chapter, I want to look at bell hooks' interpretative model of Black phallocentrism (1992) and see to what extent it can be applied to African-Caribbean boys in an inner-city boys' comprehensive. For two years I carried out intensive ethnographic field work in Township Boys school. It is situated in a middle-class suburb and the children commute from one of the most socially deprived areas of the city.

Black masculinity and phallocentricism

The term phallocentrism has its origins in French psychoanalytic theory and was later reworked into feminist discourses. Lacan (1977) and Der-rida (1987) are the originators of the term, though Derrida prefers the more language-oriented term, 'phallogocentric'. However, Lacan's theory is also about language. The best way to unpack this complex term is to look at phallocentrism as way of explaining the incessant misogyny, compul-sive heterosexuality and obsessive homophobia of many of the boys in Township school.

In bell hooks' model (1992) there is a link between the 'anxieties' of the repressed/ oppressed Black male subject and the projection of another dominant discourse. Hooks begins her narrative of Black phallocentricism with the move of Black American southerners to the North after emancipation. This massive migration also resulted in the dislocation of Black masculinity. In the Southern Black communities there were avenues for Black men to obtain respect that did not solely depend on work, money and the ability to be a provider. Hooks (1992) says:

> The extent to which a given Black man absorbed White society's notion of manhood likely determined the extent of his bitterness and despair that White supremacy continually blocked access to the patriarchal ideal. (1992, p.91)

The making of a 'Yard Man'.

For hooks, integration had a profound influence on Black gender roles and in the shaping of Black masculine dislocation. She points to a dominant perception — held by White and Black academics — of Black men as 'cut off' from a patriarchal ideal. What has not been documented are the many different types of Black males who do not feel a need to mimic White patriarchy.

The dominant perception matched the thinking of Mr Jones, the new headteacher of Township school. In terms of typologies he saw himself as antagonistic to the subculture of African- Caribbean boys. He was an African-Caribbean (born in Jamaica) who firmly believed that education is still the key force for Black social mobility. It was the only avenue open to Black people in the Caribbean and he believed passionately that education would once again free African-Caribbean children because it worked for him.

The idea that the Caribbean offered a meritocracy for Mr Jones' generation is itself questionable. As Gus John (1994) points out, there was a framework of thinking that said, 'a good education would take you out of poverty'. The reality, however, was different. These education systems were elitist and designed to cream off a certain percentage who would later run the country. The vast majority did not, and do not, have access to the quality of education that the elite class had.

Mr Jones' ideology is rooted .in this idealistic vision of Caribbean' education. It is from this perspective that he attacks the boys' subculture, which he perceives as anti-school. He is not unaware of racism, even in

23

his school, but he places the major weight of achievement on the shoulders of the boys themselves:

T.S: Do you think the new music and subculture of African-Caribbean boys helps their self-esteem?

Mr Jones: Too many of our young people prefer a Raggamuffin life because it lacks discipline and is easy. You don't get anything for nothing and if they think by living this loose Ragga type of lifestyle is going to get them anywhere — well they're wrong. Eventually you're going to have a family. How are you going to feed them? They've got to hold onto something that is concrete, something that has substance.

One of the practical steps Mr Jones took to show the boys that ragga culture must be left outside the school gates, was to ban the wearing of patterns in the boys' hair. This caused a storm, many boys saying that the policy was racist because it only affected Black boys. The hairstyle was popular when Mr Francis (the previous White Headteacher) was in charge but he never cared what hairstyle the boys wore:

T.S: Why have you banned Black boys from having patterns in their hair during term-time?

Mr Jones: No, what I am trying to do is to get them to create an atmosphere and image in the school, which is not like anywhere else. We live in a society, whether you be White or Black, where certain dress styles are stigmatised or certain types of behaviour will be associated with that dress code. Whether it's right or wrong, it's there. I want the kids in this school to use me as an example. I want to equip them with skills to manoeuvre their way through society and get to the pinnacle. As far as I am concerned it applies to their outward image as well as what comes out of their mouths. To me the whole thing comes as a package, so use me as an example and I'll guide you through so that you can get on in society.

Mr Jones sees himself as a role model — who upholds the values of one kind of African-Caribbean culture that he thinks these children are in danger of losing. He appears to be antagonistic to the values and content of the sub-culture of these children.

Mr Jones' paternalism of motivating children in accordance with his older Caribbean perspective, appeared to the children to be completely foreign. Their concept of the Caribbean is twofold, either they are not very interested or they see it as bolstering the machismo-sexism of their subculture primarily through its music. This supported Mr Jones' perception that the subculture of the boys encouraged them to look to models of behaviour that were irresponsible and destructive:

T.S: What do you think about the African-Caribbean boys' attitude to women?

Mr Jones: During a Social Education class, we were talking about children's reading books and we were trying to identify stereotypes. I told them I had ten year-old twins, one boy, one girl, and my wife and I decided we would not create this gender divide in the twins. Then one of the boys in the class said to me, 'You've only got three kids sir?' I said, 'Yes that's right.' He then replied, 'What about the others back in Jamaica?' I said, 'I've only got three children.' He said, 'Well, sir, you're not really a true Yard man!'

The term 'Yard man' is a Jamaican reference to someone who is endowed with all the stereotypical qualities of a machismo Jamaican. He is linked with a street hard-man life style and he is notorious for fathering many children with different mothers and taking no responsibilities for his actions. There is much to criticise in the actions of Mr Jones, especially his ban on patterned hairstyles, which was an important ethnic signifier for the boys. However his critique of the boys' phallocentricism is important because he challenges their essentialist perception of African-Caribbean men.

Desire and fear of Black masculinity

Hooks talks about the shift from patriarchal status to a phallocentric model. Under the patriarchal status, a man could still assert authority over his family because of tradition and Christianity. However, under advanced

25

capitalism it was the wage-earning power that determined the extent to which a man would rule over a household. Hooks (1992) then translates this into feminist terms:

> In feminist terms, this can be described as a shift from emphasis on patriarchal status (determined by one's capacity to assert power over others in a number of spheres based on maleness) to a phallocentric model, where what the male does with his penis becomes a greater and certainly a more accessible way to assert masculine status. It is easy to see how this served the interests of a capitalist state which was indeed depriving men of their rights, exploiting their labour in such a way that they only indirectly received the benefits, to deflect away from a patriarchal power based on ruling others and to emphasise a masculine status that would depend solely on the penis.

> With the emergence of a fierce phallocentrism, a man was no longer a man because he provided care for his family, he was a man simply because he had a penis. Furthermore, his ability to use that penis in the arena of sexual conquest could bring him as much status as being a wage earner and provider. A sexually defined masculine ideal rooted in physical domination and sexual possession of women could be accessible to all men. Hence, even unemployed Black men could gain status, could be seen as the embodiment of masculinity, within a phallocentric framework. (1992, p.94)

Hooks goes on to show how White men seeking alternatives to a patriarchal masculinity turned to Black men, particularly Black musicians. The idea of Black masculinity as source of envy is shown by Mac an Ghaill in the attitude of schoolboys to their African-Caribbean peers:

> Rajinder: You see there's a lot of sexuality in there. The African-Caribbeans are seen as better at football and that's really important in this school for making a reputation. And it's the same with dancing, again the Black kids are seen as the best. And the White kids and the Asians are jealous because they think that the girls will really prefer the Black kids. So, the 'race' thing gets all mixed up with other things that are important to young kids. (1994, p.86)

26

Township school was set in a part of London where one could easily experience racist attacks and yet it was known for close relationships between Black and White. This paradox came out in the youth subcultures of the school. As Hebidige (1982) shows, the impact of African-Caribbean youth culture on White youth was ambiguous but not progressive. He notes the ways in which Skinheads in the sixties incorporated Jamaican music to bolster their White nationalism. However, it is admiration of a phallocentric Black masculinity that proves to be the most disturbing in the psyche of White youths. This point is made by Les Back in his essay, 'The White Negro revisited':

> For White young men, the imaging of Black masculinity in hetero-
> sexual codes of 'hardness' and 'hypersexuality' is one of the core
> elements which attract them to Black masculine style. However, the
> image of Black sexuality as potent and 'bad' is alarmingly similar to
> racist notions of dangerous/violent 'Black muggers'. When racist
> ideas are most exposed, in situations where there is intimate contact
> between Black and White men, stereotypical ideas can be reproduced
> 'dressed up' as positive characteristics to be emulated. White identi-
> fication with Black people can become enmeshed within the discourse
> of the 'noble savage', which renders blackness exotic and reaffirms
> Black men as a 'race apart'. (1994, p.179)

When looking at Black phallocentricism there is a mirror effect on the Black male subject. He positions himself in phallocentric terms and this is confirmed by the obsessive jealousy of other groups. African-Caribbean boys are not passive subjects in the face of racialised and gendered stereotyping. They are active agents in discourses which appear to be seductively positive but are in essence racist. This leads to a strong confirmation of an identity that has its source in the dislocation of Black and White masculinity. Mac an Ghaill (1994) shows this in the contradic-tions operated by his 'African-Caribbean Macho Lads':

> They positioned themselves as sexually superior both to White and
> Asian students and to conformist Black students. More specifically,
> they spoke of themselves as the main producers of popular style,
> which they claimed made them attractive to young women. This could
> not be simply read in terms of youthful boasting. The African Carib-
> beans appropriated discursive themes from dominant ambivalent

27

White student representations, in which Black male students' behaviour was over-sexualized. As for some White male teachers, this consisted of contradictory cultural investments, of desire and jealousy in the highly exaggerated ascription to the Black Macho Lads of stylish resistance, sporting skills and 'having a reputation with girls'. (1994 p 87)

This analysis shows that Black masculinity is a subordinated masculinity shaped by many contradictions. The internalisation and incorporation of the dominant definitions of masculinity has arisen in order to contest conditions of dependency, racism and powerlessness. Phallocentrism is an attempt to recuperate some degree of power influence under the subordinated conditions created by racism. Staples (1982) calls this the development of the 'Macho' or 'dual dilemma'. Mercer describes this process as a...

form of misdirected or "negative" resistance, as it is shaped by the challenge to the hegemony of the socially dominant White male, yet assumes a form which is in turn oppressive to Black women, children and indeed, to Black men themselves as it can entail self-destructive acts and attitudes. (1994 p.143)

The machismo in the music

So far, I have shown how hooks' model reveals the way some disenfranchised Black males, across the diaspora, contest their own oppression by adopting a sexist phallocentrism. However, unlike Staples (1982), she does not accept that this is a 'natural' position to take; for her it is an easy option, which is ultimately self-destructive. In hooks' view (1994), what has made Black phallocentrism so seductive is the way White capitalism through the music industry has made it a million dollar industry:

Where is the anger and rage at females expressed in this music coming from, the glorification of all acts of violence? These are the difficult questions that Staples feels no need to answer.

One cannot answer them honestly without placing accountability on larger structures of domination (sexism, racism, class, elitism) and the individuals — often White, usually male, but not always — who are hierarchically placed to maintain and perpetuate the values that

28

uphold these exploitative and oppressive systems. That means taking a critical look at the politics of hedonistic consumerism, the values of the men and women who produce gangster rap. It would mean considering the seduction of young Black males who find that they can make more money producing lyrics that promote violence, sexism, misogyny than with any other content. How many disenfranchised Black males would not surrender to expressing virulent forms of sexism if they knew the rewards would be unprecedented material power and fame? (1994, p.117)

This view is supported by Onyekachi Wambu, writing in *The Voice*:

The second reason why I worry about the new sex in Black music is because of the way it has become just another commodity. I think we have crossed the thin line between celebrating sex, in the tradition of the best of Black music and exploiting bodies to sell sex. (1994, p.13)

Writing in the *Sunday Times* (February 13, 1994) Betty Lowenthal comments on how Black women are tired of the misogynist rap lyrics of rappers like Snoop Doggy Dogg:

'I got sunshine, on a cloudy day/ I got an AK 47's gonna blow you away/ Just another day in South Central L.A./ with my hoe (whore) ...'

'Hoes', 'Bitches', Ak 47s (automatic rifles) and even gang banging are commonplace in the lyrics of gangsta rap artists such as Snoop, Ice Cube and Dr Dread. The controversy surrounds not only the lyrics of Snoop's album but the packaging: a high art sleeve features a 'bitch' — an enormous chested Black woman depicted with an exaggerated rear end complete with tail sticking out of a kennel. (1994, p.14)

One of the consequences of the idealisation of a phallocentric Black masculinity expressed in popular Black music is a critique, mainly from Black feminists and gays, that accuses Black men of inventing another form of oppression. Mercer describes it as a 'hideous ambivalence'; he says:

Sociologists like Robert Staples (1982) have long since recognised this paradox in their accounts of Black male gender 'roles'. Staples sees machismo, for example, as an inherently conflictual psychosex-

29

ual formation in which subordinate men internalise normative ideals of patriarchal power and privilege to win a degree of self-empowerment over the powerlessness that White supremacy entails. And yet, when men of colour aspire to dominate others also subjected to the same system of power and control, the emptiness of the circular concept of 'internalisation' is revealed: it constantly misrecognises the unconscious identifications at stake in ideological struggles over representation of 'self' and the 'other'. (1994 p 140)

Gilroy (1993) and Mercer (1994) have shown the negative way the subculture acts on Black men through the 'internalisation of stereotypes'. Bell hooks and other Black feminist writers share these concerns and point to music lyrics in particular as an inspiration for misogynist attitudes.

Hooks points to the embracing of patriarchy and phallocentrism as not only destructive in relationships with Black women, but as even more so with Black males:

If Black men no longer embraced phallocentric masculinity, they would be empowered to explore their fear and hatred of other men, learning new ways to relate. How many Black men will have to die before Black folks are willing to look at the link between the contemporary plight of Black men and their continued allegiance to patriarchy and phallocentrism. (1994, p.112)

In an article, 'A Feminist analysis of the Defence of Obscene Rap Lyrics', Sonja Peterson-Lewis (1991) adapts the work of Mary Daly (1973) in her book *Beyond God and the Father*. Daly points to the myth of Eve in the Bible as responsible for rationalising the misogyny in popular culture. Patterson-Lewis takes up this theme and applies it to Black male attitudes in *Rap and Ragga* (1991):

Daly, too says that the creation of 'otherness' is central to adopting a dominating and manipulative posture toward people. With the assigning of women to the role of the gullible, greed-driven counterpart of men whose yielding to temptation ruined life for all of humanity, the stage was set for making women scapegoats for a variety of evils in the world. This myth is so pervasive in popular culture that it also appears to fuel the seeming misogyny found in some rap music. (1991, p.73)

An example of this misogyny comes from the lyrics of 2 Live Crew's rap *Dick Almighty,* where we hear the words:

I'll tear a pussy open cause it's satisfaction
The bitch won't leave cause it's fatal attraction
Dick so powerful she'll kneel and pray.

And in the rap titled 'Put Her in the Buck,' the group teaches young males a 'new' sexual technique supposedly 'done by the masters'. The third verse shows that this technique is pleasurable to men but painful to women: 'I'll break you down and dick you long / Bust your pussy and break your backbone'. Or, finally in '2 Live Blues', the Crew raps: 'Come lay your Black ass down right beside me / while a grab a little bit of pussy.'

In contrast, Henry Louis Gates (1990) argues for a positive angle on the relationship between popular rap music and Black masculinity. He says:

These young artists are acting out to a lively dance music, a parodic exaggeration of the age-old stereotypes of the oversexed Black female and male. Their exuberant use of the hyperbole (phantasmagoric sexual organs for example) undermines — for anyone fluent in Black cultural codes — a too literal minded hearing of lyrics.

Gates insists that Black youth culture should be interpreted within the context of Black culture generally and 'signifying' specifically. To signify is to subvert the master narrative by a coded exchange:

Just as Blacks have 'imitated' White Western languages, literatures, religions, music, dance, dress and family life, but with a critical 'signifying' difference, so shall Afro-American literary criticism steal the meat from the sandwich but leave the White bread untouched. (1990, p.235-236)

Patterson-Lewis feels that to credit rap groups like 2 Live Crew with having the literary genius of satirists is to overstate their case. For her, their obsession with sex is used as a violent weapon against women:

Overall, the lyrics lack the wit and strategic use of subtle social commentary necessary for effective satire, thus, they do not so much debunk myths as create new ones, the major one being that in interacting with Black women, 'anything goes'. These lyrics not only fail to satirize 'the myth of the hypersexed Black', they also commit the moral blunder of sexualizing the victimisation of women, Black women in particular (1991, p.78)

She goes on to dismiss any justification for profane lyrics and highlights not only the damaging affects this has on the image of Black males but also the role of the media in perpetuating these images. Commenting on the controversial rap group, 2 Live Crew, the first music group to be charged in an American court for obscene lyrics, she says:

> 2 Live Crew's lyrics not only desensitise their audiences to violence against women, they also help to rationalise and reinforce a nihilistic mentality among those who already suffer from the effects of ghetto reality. Finally their lyrics help to rationalise an already existent suspicion and distrust of Black males. The study of the media's potential to affect public and private behaviour and attitudes should continue unimpeded by the trivialist, particularist, spiritualist, and universalist arguments posited by those who wish to veil their economic aspirations under the label of art. (1991, p.78)

For Patterson-Lewis, it is the commodification of a certain kind of Black music that is disturbing and she argues that the very success of this product is rooted in an exploitation of the wider social and economic problems facing Black men across the Diaspora. In the end this culture or 'market opportunity' fails to provide a critique of the deeper conditions that have caused the marginalisation of Black males. Rather it reinforces those same conditions.

Mike has gathered many of his ideas about Black masculinity not only from inside school but from outside, namely through music. He shows this when he talks about the music and lyrics he listens to:

T.S: What have you got on your bedroom walls?

Mike: On my wall I have all my sporting certificates and then on another wall I have music artists like Ninjaman.

T.S: What do you like about Ninjaman ?

Mike: I like the way he cusses other DJs. He's got his kind of style and he speaks a lot of badness. He speaks about guns and killing people. Kids like the way he swears.

> Most Black boys in school rate Ninja because he doesn't care what he says. He's a rebel.

T.S: What do you think of the calls to have this kind of music banned?

Mike: A lot of White people are scared of Black people, of the hard image of the rappers. That's why it shouldn't be banned.

It is impossible to prove that listening to Ninjaman will make you become a disruptive pupil. In fact, as Mike has said, Ninjaman was popular amongst most of the African-Caribbean students, who of course included those who were conformists at school. However, these cultural icons had a profound influence with the students who felt powerless in the schooling process. Many of them were members of the school gang called 'The Posse'. 'The Posse' included students who were poor readers, those who had disruptive home lives and students who felt aggrieved because of teacher racism. Ninjaman, the icon of Black masculine phallus, is the inspiration against a schooling culture these students partially want to reject. Hooks would argue that some of the African-Caribbean boys 'colonised the symbolic spaces' within the school with the hallmark of a destructive Black machismo.

Township school and Black masculinity

If hooks' interpretative model of phallocentrism can be applied to Township school, there must be evidence of what Mercer calls the 'dual dilemma'; in other words a 'Machismo' based on the misdirection of negative resistance. Mike Henry is a core member of 'The Posse'. He has one of the worst exclusion rates in the school, mainly for violent clashes with teachers and students. He was very much aware of how much power his 'tough image' had in Township:

T.S: Do you belong to a gang or posse?

Mike: We have a group in school but the real gang meets outside school called the Jungle City Boys. Some kids from this school belong to this gang. We go around doing graffiti and mucking around. We go looking for girls.

T.S: How do other students see you?

Mike: I think that see me as tough because I try not to act as a wimp.

T.S: How would you describe a wimp?

Mike: Someone like my cousin Jeff Taylor, he avoids going to tuck, he avoids going to lunch, even though he wants to go. Another one is Dennis. He came in the first year with the reputation as a bad fighter. He's just a pussy, a woman, who walks away from fights. And he's always grovelling to the teachers. I hate him.

T.S: What do you feel teachers think about you?

Mike: They're always going on about my size. I know some of the weak teachers are really frightened of me. They are even scared of my Dad. One day I had a big argument on the stairs with Mr Fletcher. He told me that if I threatened him that he would get his own Mafia on me. I told this to my Dad who came down the school. When Mr Fletcher heard he had come, he ran out of school jumped in his car and ran off. My Dad would never hurt anyone; he just wanted to talk to the teacher about my behaviour. I think they are scared of Black people.

Mike, like some African-Caribbean boys in Township, perceived being pro-school as unmanly. Jeff Taylor is not a real man because he does not get into trouble with the teachers. It is in a sexual framework that Mike describes his position and how he has been positioned. He dismisses conformist students as 'pusses', compared to his confrontational approach. He complains that the teachers are always referring to his size — which was a continual problem for many African-Caribbean boys — this illustrates the White teachers' obsession with Black bodies. This division of 'mind' and 'body' is what Connell calls 'differentiated masculinities'. He argues that:

The differentiation of masculinities occurs in relation to a school curriculum which organises knowledge hierarchically and sorts students into an academic hierarchy. By institutionalising academic

34

failure via competitive grading and streaming, the school forces differentiation on the boys. But masculinity is organised on the macro scale — around social power. Social power in terms of access to higher education, entry to professions, command of communication, is being delivered to boys who are academic 'successes'. The reaction of the 'failed' is likely to be a claim to other sources of power, even other definitions of masculinity. Sporting prowess, physical aggression, sexual conquest may do. (1987, p.292)

In Township school, members of 'The Posse' (a gang of African-Caribbean fifteen-year-olds) all felt that the schooling system had failed them. So was their status enhanced, as Staples has suggested, by a shift to extreme forms of masculine domination? Eric has a long record of exclusions, mostly over bullying other children. He had just come back from another exclusion, this time for aggressive behaviour and forcefully taking the dinner money from a first year student. He says that most of the members of 'The Posse' have outgrown school and find it difficult to be treated as 'little kids' when outside. They hang out with 'big people':

T.S: Why do you think that you've clashed so many times with the teachers?

Eric: I admit I've done some bad things but what really annoys me is that they treat me like I'm a baby. They're always talking down to me. Kids are having kids and we know how to make money from early. Teachers are treating us like little kids, even when our parents don't treat us like this.

T.S: Does this include the new Headmaster?

Eric: Well Mr Jones — he was born in Jamaica. He has got an understanding. But times have changed. He's seeing it in his time. Even though it might be harder in his day we're going through a different phase.

T.S: Tell me about that change?

Eric: Kids from 13 upwards know about sex. They cuss. They sleep with loads of girls. They're doing more things than Mr Jones could ever dream about.

Eric rejects school not because it is too White and middle-class but because it cannot meet his expectations as a 'man'. Although he is sympathetic to Mr Jones, the headteacher's brand of respectable conservative ideology is, for Eric, out of touch with his own perception of manhood. His perception is not based on ideas of 'responsibility' and 'caring' but is rooted in two actions: the ability to make money and babies. Eric's father has eight children from four different women and is separated from Eric's mother. I asked him if he felt he was likely to end up the same way:

> Eric: Well at the moment I've got four girlfriends and although they don't know about each other, I'm smart enough to use a condom. I won't have any children until I make my money. If any of them have a baby for me I'll make sure that I give them money for my child.

Eric still perceives 'manhood' in a money/sex dynamic. He talks about his responsibilities as an extension of his dream to be wealthy. It is an immature vision, especially because he has no real job plans outside of the long shot of becoming a professional footballer. So he characterisese a scenario which was typical of the boys in 'The Posse'. They felt that the schooling process assaulted the thing that was most precious to them — their 'manhood'. The teachers' ability to 'shame them up' and 'make them look small' was the reason for many conflicts. This perception of manhood also extended into the fear that many teachers had of the 'size', 'presence' and 'styles of walking' of members of 'The Posse'. It was this that they felt was the source of repression in Township and they responded with their own exaggerated sexuality. Delroy, like Eric, had a long record of exclusions. He was often seen on the corridor during lesson time, where he listens to music tapes with other members of 'The Posse'. He has an essentialist perception of Black people which links them not with academic success but only with pleasure seeking:

> T.S: Which group of children would you say gets the most exclusions?
>
> Delroy: Black
>
> T.S: Why?
>
> Delroy: Because that's the way Black people are.

T.S: What do you mean?

Delroy: Well if you look at Indians they work hard and own shops, Black people are into other stuff.

T.S: What other stuff?

Delroy: They got more social life. They go out more. Black people aren't thinking about work. They've got other things on their mind.

T.S: What other things have you got on your mind?

Delroy: Just getting out of school, meeting my friends and having a good time.

T.S: Are you saying that Black kids in this school don't want to work?

Delroy: No they just like to express themselves. Show everyone who they are. A lot of my friends don't like to be told what to do. They hate being given orders. If a teacher tells them to do something and they don't respect the teacher, they're going to turn round and tell them to shut up.

Delroy reveals a platonic conflict between the body and the mind. The way in which these boys have been gendered within the school context has left them not only alienated from 'caring' and 'responsible' notions of masculinity but also as victims of the commodification of Black culture. This is an argument that Gilroy develops in his book, *Small Acts*:

The popularity of materialism and misogyny is partly a result of the fact that those images of blackness are the mechanisms of the 'cross-over' relationship. They are in a sense the most comfortable representations of blackness. They are the images that the dominant culture finds easiest to accept, process and take pleasure in. So often the medium of their transmission is a discourse on Black masculinity that constructs Black men as both sources of pleasure and sources of danger to White listeners and spectators. (1993, p.35)

Ms Williams, a Black teacher at Township school, shifts the responsibility for the school's high exclusion rate of African-Caribbean boys away from teachers and directly to the 'machismo' subculture of the boys. She says:

> Many African-Caribbean parents find it hard to accept that the reason for the disproportionate number of excluded African-Caribbean boys rests solely on the fact that African-Caribbean boys are more likely to do things that warrant exclusion.
>
> My evidence for this is based on the attitude and behaviour of the African-Caribbean boys who I went to school with and that of those in this school. Though it pains me, as an African-Caribbean myself, to admit that the exclusions of African-Caribbean pupils are based solely on the attitude of the pupils themselves, I feel even more strongly that to deny this fact is more destructive in both the short and the long term.
>
> The African-Caribbean community is so obsessed with trying to prove that teachers and schools are racist instead of trying to work out strategies to ensure success for African-Caribbean pupils, despite the system — then it will be energy and time well spent. What is less documented are the reasons why African-Caribbean males feel the need to misbehave in ways that will ensure ultimate exclusion. This image is based on their physique, the way they speak and also on their perceived culture: the rap, the dress, the films, the posters. In fact this image is totally incorrect. African-Caribbean males are actually very insecure.

Although Ms Williams has underestimated the influence of teacher racism in Township school, she confirms hooks' analysis that marginalised masculinity, when subject to racism, leads some African-Caribbean boys to adopt a phallocentrism they feel has been denied to them.

Phallocentrism: rebelling into conformity

Subcultures worked on two levels; on the one side it confirmed a rich complex ethnicity, which benefited the African-Caribbean boys in making their social identity. This ethnicity was not 'fixed' or 'natural', it was an artifice which incorporated multiple influences from around the diaspora as well as reworking themes from the past. In this sense clothes, music and hairstyles become ethnic and political signifiers. It is from this position that a 'politics of resistance' has its roots. The subcultures around the Black Power era of the sixties and the Rastafarian movement of the seventies, are important examples of how Black youth have retained their self-esteem and challenged the authority of White dominance.

On the negative side, hooks' model of Black phallocentrism shows that both on the level of street subculture and in the scholarship of Black nationalism there is a self-destructive discourse that seeks to replace a White dominant patriarchy with a Black phallocentricism. She says:

Black men and women who espouse cultural nationalism continue to see the struggle for Black liberation largely as a struggle to recover Black manhood. In her essay 'Africa On my Mind: Gender, Counter Discourse and African American Nationalism', E. Frances White shows that overall Black nationalist perspectives on gender are rarely rooted purely in the Afrocentric logic they seek to advance, but rather reveal their ties to White paradigms: 'In making appeals to conservative notions of appropriate gender behaviour, African-American nationalists reveal their ideological ties to other nationalist movements, including European and Euro-American bourgeois nationalists over the past 200 years. These parallels exist despite the different class and power base of these movements'. (1992, p.106-107)

It is in this sense that the ethnic signals from some of the boys, such as members of 'The Posse', offers a destructive way of thinking. Its only logic is the offensive language of misogyny, homophobia or hyper-heterosexuality.

The question of how this negative aspect of subculture influences schooling, must be seen in the context of a schooling system that seeks to make African-Caribbean boys intellectually powerless and/or bodily powerful. In this sense the conflict between Foster and Gillborn makes no sense (see Gillborn, 1995). They are both right. Foster (1990) is right when he says that the reason why African-Caribbean children are failing is that too many are going to bad schools. These are schools that are failing in terms of exam results, discipline and leadership. Gillborn (1990) is also right when he says that in many schools African-Caribbean boys suffer from the myth of an 'African-Caribbean challenge', which has a sexual dimension.

For Skeggs, this sexual dimension within education is characterised by different methods of regulation. Drawing on the work of Foucault, she says:

> The first Foucault (1970) identifies as the internal discourse of the institution. Historically, he argues, the organisation of education was predicated upon the assumption that sexuality existed, that it was precocious, active and ever present. The second method of regulation involves the process of inclusion and delegitimation of certain forms of sexuality alongside inclusion and control of others ... The third mechanism of regulation involves the prioritising of masculinity as norm through the organisational structure and pedagogy of education. Taken together the process of regulation and normalisation provide an interpretative framework of discourses of sexuality in a grid of possibilities which students draw from and are located. (1991, p.128-129)

The framework of discourses confronting African-Caribbean boys in Township school were varied. There was a fear and an envy of African-Caribbean boys from White youths (who envied their reputation as 'fighters' and 'fuckers'). It also came from the teachers who saw this subculture as threat to order and their perception of the ideal pupil. It is this, along with the general failing of the school (discipline, resources) which gave these boys a phallocentric framework in which they located themselves.

The African-Caribbean boys in Township responded to this framework in two ways. The first was an incorporation of a phallocentric perspective. Basically this was to glory in the stereotypes of Black masculinity and use them as a means not only to resist schooling but also to oppress Black conformist students with a sexualized discourse. Therefore Black boys who worked hard were considered 'batty men' (gay) or 'pussies' (effeminate).

The other choice, adopted by the conformists, was to try and accommodate the anti-school demands of 'The Posse' and at the same time conform to school rules and work practices. Fuller (1980), in her study of Black girls, talks about their ability to accommodate aspects of schooling without the loss of face amongst their peer groups. In Township school, too many African-Caribbean boys were unable to perform this juggling act. The phallocentric response became the easier option.

If researchers are to challenge racism successfully, there needs to be an understanding of how the racialised subject is gendered. There is a need to go beyond additive models of oppression and look at complex matrices of power relations, bringing together critical sociological and psychological frameworks. This will also mean schools giving up their coyness when it comes to looking at Black male sexuality.

Chapter 3

Why Muslim girls are more feminist in Muslim schools

Kaye Haw

This chapter examines how the discourses of gender and 'race' are articulated in the educational experiences of Muslim girls and focuses on the assumptions that are made when racism and sexism are viewed as a dichotomy. It draws upon the data from my research in a private Muslim girls' school (Old Town High) and a single-sex state school with a high proportion of Muslim girls (City State) with a good reputation as far as its equal opportunities policy and multicultural initiatives are concerned.[1]

City State draws its students from a geographically diverse area and is staffed mainly by White, non-Muslim teachers. There are three South Asian members of staff, one the male Urdu teacher (and the only Muslim), and two female Section 11 teachers. Old Town High, on the other hand, is situated in the heart of the locality from where it draws its students so the parents are able, and feel able, to visit the school at any time to discuss their concerns. All the staff in this school are female and half are Muslims.

The chapter is divided into four sections. The first provides a brief background to the case studies and a methodological placing and evaluation of them. The second section gives a brief overview of feminisms, concentrating specifically on poststructuralism and feminism and how they have impacted on education and educational issues in this country. The third concerns itself with the case studies. In the light of this analysis the final section considers why the Muslim girls in this Muslim school are more likely to be more feminist than the Muslim girls in the state school.

The Theoretical Perspective

This section focuses on the theoretical perspectives and principles upon which this research is based. For me, the research began with a fundamental question of whether I should be doing a piece of research with Muslim women who have a background in Pakistan when I am a White, not formally religious, middle class woman who cannot write beyond her own discursive positionings.

Given that racism is a White problem, there will be White people who wish to research in this area. When 'race' is considered, the focus is invariably on 'Black' peoples, its victims, who are thereby constructed as the 'other', the 'problem'. By asking the question, how White privilege and power is exercised (and examining the mechanisms whereby this power is exercised) it should be possible to gain a better understanding of the processes of racial oppression and racism. This is the perspective of the research.

The research involves a community, which feels itself to be oppressed, and girls within that community who feel that, for many reasons, the element of choice and decision making is taken away from them. At the same time 'race' is not always experienced in a negative way but provides also a positive context for celebration, in the same way that Islam and what it is to be a Muslim woman are celebrated. Certainly the lives of the Muslim women who participated in this research are multi-faceted and often tempered by a recognition of material and other constraints.

The analytical perspective adopted, therefore, has been shaped principally by ideas within feminism and poststructuralism. This allows for an exploration of how Muslim girls and women position themselves in discourses that subordinate them and a consideration of the workings of patriarchal structures such as schools and education generally (Weiner,

1994). It additionally provides an analytical framework for examining the micro-political — that is, how power is exercised at local levels, how oppression works and is experienced, and where resistances are possible. The aim is to construct theory which combines perspectives which deal with fragmentation, hybridity and pluralism, with critical perspectives which centre on ownership, empowerment and open, focused interactions with concrete others (Benhabib, 1992; Shackleton, 1993).

The research design incorporated both a qualitative and a quantitative element. The interviews with the staff, headteachers, ex-students and parents were semi-structured. Those with the staff were focused around the advantages and disadvantages of their school; the issue of single-sex education; what they felt were the aims of education for girls; the needs of their students, specifically their Muslim students; and equal opportunities. Each interview was preceded by the presentation of a set of photographs portraying different school situations, which the participant was asked to interpret freely.

The work with the students took a different form. They were asked to complete three questionnaires. The first questionnaire, partly based on the work of Horner (1972) and Faulkner (1991), took the form of the completion of an imaginative story. The second was a basic attitude survey concerning the rights and roles of women in contemporary society. The third questionnaire was aimed more specifically at asking the students about their school, whether they would like to change schools and why, what they felt their needs were; and what they wanted to do when they left school. The students were also interviewed informally in groups. Initially, this took the form of discussions around the same set of photographs shown to the staff. This is the basis for this chapter and its analysis.

Feminisms in Education

The purpose of this section is to give a brief overview of the perspectives which weave their way through the history of feminism and to concentrate on a particular aspect of feminist theory — that relating to education. A detailed consideration of the wealth of contemporary international work on feminist epistemology and its arguments and current debates, is beyond the scope of this chapter. However, such theories of feminism and education reflect the broader fundamental feminist concerns of patriarchy, capitalism, power relationships, biology, the body, physical strength and violence, sexuality and sexual violence. Before highlighting the fragmentations of feminism in relation to education, I want to emphasise the commonalties which thread their way through these feminisms.

Firstly, all feminisms emphasise the centrality of gender divisions to the organisation of society and its mode of operation. Secondly, all these feminist epistemologies have a moral/ political stance, with 'values' and 'power' as organising concepts and all have been developed in response to the disempowerment of women which forms the basis of other epistemologies (Griffiths, 1995a). Feminism is not just about theory. It is about our day to day lives and realities.

This relates to a third uniting factor: that of the importance of self or subjectivity. Feminist epistemologies do not assume that there is an 'objective', 'view from nowhere' and all assume that the self or subjectivity is a starting point in the collective enterprise of formulating a feminist perspective (Griffiths, 1995a).

These commonalities provide the starting point for charting the development of feminist discourses within and about British education. They correspond to Weiner's three dimensions of feminism which are:

Political — a movement to improve the conditions and life-chances for girls and women; Critical — a sustained intellectual critique of dominant (male) forms of knowing and doing; Praxis-orientated — concerned with the development of more ethical forms of professional and personal practice. (1994, p.7-8)

Such similarities should be kept in mind as I consider the feminist perspectives which are of theoretical significance, because they affect opinions concerning educational outcomes and strategies for change. The following account necessarily reduces and distils different feminist theoretical approaches to education to their essence through 'categorisation'. (Connell, 1987).

This was less problematical in the seventies and eighties when Jaggar (1983) identified four different kinds of White, western feminisms: liberal, marxist, radical and socialist. However, the 1990s has witnessed a merging and multipositioning of these perspectives in the light of post-structuralist and postmodernist influences. These trends can be traced clearly in feminist academic texts concerned with educational issues, especially if their date of publication is noted.

In 1989 Tong identified seven — liberal, marxist, radical, psycho-analytic, socialist, existentialist and postmodernism feminisms. Adopting a poststructural analysis of feminisms in education, Weiner (1994) also mentions these, plus Christian feminism, humanist feminism, Muslim feminism and eco-feminism, which have emerged as feminism has become more fractured, and identity politics more possible. In this respect 'Black' feminism, in particular, has been responsible for causing feminists to re-evaluate their thinking (Amos and Parmar, 1984; Mirza, 1992; Wright, 1987 and Williams, 1987). This work has also highlighted the way that the treatment of 'race' and gender as a duality has rendered 'Black' girls invisible.

It is, arguably, liberal and radical feminisms which have particularly permeated and influenced the British school curriculum and educational practices more generally, in terms of the development of equal opportunities policies to ensure equality of access in educational settings and in making the educational experiences of women more central to the curriculum. Marxist and socialist feminism have also impacted on educational theory through their focus on the educational experiences of working class girls.

Other feminisms appear to have had less impact on education although poststructuralism, principally through the work of Walkerdine (1990) in Britain, is becoming influential. The interest in the way that discourse operates as a 'normalising' process in which knowledge and power are connected, and the prioritisation of the 'micro', means that it is possible to create a reverse-discourse, thus creating alternative ways to say the unsayable. Schools, teaching/learning relationships and curriculum texts are made up of many different and often contradictory discourses which are systematically related. The positioning of an individual with regard to these differing and competing discourses can be said to be discursive: that is, individuals can be discursively placed with reference to a number of discourses and be situated in a number of ways. This opens up possibilities for individuals actively to take up a range of ways of being and seeing.

It is this flexibility which I believe provides an analytically useful tool for this chapter and its concern to theorise the differing experiences of Muslim students in different schools. Each school can be seen to consist of fragile and fluid sets of competing discourses, some of which are dominant, some subordinate, some peacefully co-existing, some struggling for ascendancy (Kenway et al, 1994). The individuals within each school are discursively placed to challenge and change the struggle over meaning.

I have already pointed out the weaknesses of categorisation; however, this analysis does show how feminism has shifted over the past two decades and how this has impacted on education and educational issues. At the beginning of this section I emphasised the commonalities running through these different feminisms. Feminism is about resistance to any one dominant discourse but the distinctions are helpful to the focus of this chapter and its thesis that Muslim girls are more feminist in Muslim schools.

The Case Studies

Each case study generated a wealth of data but this section necessarily concentrates on one of the dominant issues which emerged from the perceptions of the staff and the students themselves.[2]

Keeping to the focus of the primary research questions

The 'way in' to such an overwhelming array of data was through the perception of the staff and students in each school of their experiences of single-sex schooling and what they saw as the advantages and disadvantages of their particular schools.

Some common ground emerged between the two schools over the issues of single-sex schooling. It was seen to provide an atmosphere free from male dominance and harassment, to provide equal access to the curriculum both during lessons and in terms of subject choice and to provide encouragement in terms of positive role models. A strongly emerging category from both schools was that of feelings of 'sisterhood' between staff, staff and pupils, and pupils. It was felt that this in turn led to a warm, friendly, supportive and non-threatening atmosphere. It is from this base that pupils felt they had the freedom to explore ideas about being a woman, or specifically, in the case of the Muslim school, a Muslim woman.

This atmosphere was perceived to lead to feelings of confidence and assertiveness for the non-Muslim students in City State and the Muslim students of Old Town High but not necessarily for the Muslim students of City State who, significantly, did not mention such feelings in their replies. The following is typical of comments from the staff in City State:

> *They (the Muslim students) also tend to be the ones who've got less confidence.* I think they don't aim high. I feel they're quieter and they need confidence in the class to speak up because other students can be louder than they are. (CS) (emphasis added)

The staff also were concerned about the resultant difficulties of this lack of confidence in encouraging the Muslim students to participate in lessons.

> The Asian group of girls, usually, given a choice, will tend to work together and resent being ungrouped. Sometimes I will mix the entire class up. I often find then that if you get one or two Asian girls in a group with other girls, the couple of Asian girls will tend to go extremely quiet, more quiet than they are normally and not join in, not contribute even to discussion. Just do as they're told, as it were. (CS)

On this issue another teacher commented:-

> They won't read aloud. I don't mean they are intimidated in the sense of bullying, just a presence. CS

One ex-pupil felt that she had been allowed 'to drift away' at school. She attributed this to her non-confrontational behaviour and lack of confidence, which meant that she was allowed to coast along in lessons. The less she felt the teachers encouraged her, the more she drifted away.[3] Significantly, as with the non-Muslim girls in City State, comments concerning the advantages of being educated in a single-sex girls' school — in terms of the encouragement that they were given to be confident and assertive so that they could express their own opinions and be women — emerged strongly in the replies of the students of Old Town High:

> I like the environment of my school and the way the teachers push you to do your utmost to make you produce the results you want, although I don't agree with too much pressurising. In this school I like the way some teachers think of you as an individual and not a whole class. They make you work and try to build your confidence, make you realise that what you do does matter. It is relevant and your

future relies on it. Since I have been to this school I have learned a lot, not just about education, but about life: how it could change. I have gained a lot of confidence although I am sometimes a bit too confident, which I shouldn't be. (OTH)

This comment is of interest for two reasons. Firstly, because this student expresses her gratitude at being treated as an individual. This contrasts sharply with the experiences of the Muslim students in City State because they, like other students belonging to ethnic minority groups, appeared to be treated as a group rather than as individuals. This was in contrast with their White peers. Secondly, because her confidence is obviously causing her some confusion and possible difficulties.

It became evident from the analysis at this point that clear differences began to emerge between the two schools in terms of: an emphasis on religion and a strong moral framework; an emphasis on academic performance; questions of confidence and assertiveness, possibly linked to self-knowledge; and a sense of cultural identity.

Both schools emphasised the need to encourage their students to be self-confident, correctly assertive young women who would make a positive contribution to the community and as mothers of the next generation. However one of the marked differences is pertinent to the focus of this chapter. It stems from the fact that Old Town High needs not only to prove itself to society at large but also to the local and wider Muslim communities. Whereas City State has a commitment to overturn the stereotype of what it means to be woman, Old Town High has a commitment to overturn the stereotype of what it means to be a Muslim woman and one who attended a Muslim school. One of the ways it believes it can do this is through academic achievement. In this school, academic achievement was encouraged through the provision of an environment where the girls felt secure enough in their own identity to question, challenge and assert their rights as Muslim women and actively to pursue further and higher education.[4]

The commitment to gender issues and to challenging traditional, stereotypical gender roles emerged very strongly throughout this part of the analysis, in both schools. It is here that the staff in City State voiced some concern that, although they were committed to ensuring that their students challenged and questioned and analysed gender issues, at the same time they were 'treading on the cultural toes' of their Muslim students and,

50

perhaps more importantly, their parents. The following is typical of these concerns:

The responsibilities that they are expected to take on at home do, to a large extent, colour their view of the future. It certainly colours the idea the parents have of what we should be providing for them in terms of curriculum. They are expected to learn how to make a home and look after a family as the first priority rather than as in addition to their career. It is a difficult one because you've got to be able to value the Muslim part of that student and all that that culture can give as a community. It's a very, very hard line to hold, I think, to give them a sense of their own individuality and worth and yet also value their culture and what that means for them and their families. (CS)

Tensions were identified in the responses of the staff of City State as they tried to reconcile their desire to encourage the students to challenge and question the stereotypes of women; their rights and their roles in contemporary society on the one hand, whilst giving due consideration to what they understood to be the religious/cultural beliefs of the Muslim students on the other hand. It is at this point that the discourses of 'race' and gender articulate on a daily and very real basis. The staff in City State did not feel 'comfortable' in this area. They used terms like 'fall into the pit' 'wary about being pushy' and 'worry about saying the wrong thing'. Davis (1984) argues that many western feminist teachers do see a counter position between opposing sexism in school and opposing racism, and are inclined to give priority to the former. If this is so, it is not without considerable 'liberal angst' on the part of the staff in City State who, feeling less comfortable with the 'race' aspect of the situation, often seem to give this priority.

I don't want to stereotype to be quite honest. I believe this school and the home conflict. I feel, *I didn't fall into the pit,* but I was aware of going to ask the questions of 'what are you doing when you leave here?', 'what would you like to do?', and I learned to maybe put these questions in a different light or not assume that they were going to do anything. I find that when you are in a smaller group, when I do course work with them, they ask about me. *You give a little bit, but I feel that I would not say things to them that I would say to a White girl or a Black girl because I couldn't say that my husband does the dishes —*

or I feel I don't want to because that could create problems. (CS) (emphasis added)

In this instance the racism/sexism contradiction is very clear.

Such comments often prefaced perceptions that inevitably such clashes of expectation led to tensions, conflicts and dilemmas.

> I often feel as though I am in a dilemma. It's this *dichotomous* situation where you feel as though the school is leading the girls along one path, and it can be at a tangent to what is actually required of them at home. *It's presenting what is available without offending parental opinions, really.* That's a difficulty, reaching a balance. You have to be aware, *you've got to be on your toes all the time.* (CS) (emphasis added)

The staff of City State also referred to the difficulties that they believed the Muslim students encountered at being confronted on a daily basis with western cultural norms. They believed that this not only meant that they questioned and felt resentment at their own cultural restrictions but were not able to discuss this, either amongst themselves because of community pressure, or with other students or staff from outside the community.

> I think the Muslim girls see the freedom, as they always see it, of what a lot of the girls have outside of school and they're sometimes feeling a resentment that they can't have that same freedom. They form little support groups amongst themselves naturally. I mean I think it's forced to be so. It's a very close-knit cultural group. I think perhaps they are aware that they sometimes have to be careful what they're saying in case someone passed it on to mum or a brother, or someone heard. They will go along with all the things such as going home late — that sort of thing; they'll go along with what they think I want from them or what they think the other girls will want from them as well. I think they're very careful not to bring their own cultural issues into the lesson because I don't think they want to be mocked and sometimes I don't know how much to encourage them because they do get mocked when they do it. (CS)

The tensions illustrated by these comments are also echoed in the replies of the students. In City State, the Muslim students commented on the gap between school and home and talked about pressure, stress, confusion and not knowing who to listen to.

Yes, because it is different, because you don't know what to do because you can't make your mind up what to do: what your mum and dad say or your teachers say. (CS)

What the school tells us about male and female differences is not the same as I have at home. My family have typical views about men but I do not get confused because I know that they are wrong so I know how to react with these things in the future. (CS)

Yes there is. My family says something else and teachers say something. This causes me pressure and confusion. (CS)

Yes, it does create a gap between myself and my home and sometimes I get confused. (CS)

Yes, when you go home after school on days you get so stressed and you can't do things you want to do. (CS)

In contrast, the Muslim girls in Old Town High said that no gap was created and commented on (i) feeling comfortable at being in an all Muslim and an all girls' school; (ii) the fact that they learnt about Islam and were able to perform their religious observances without feeling in any way out of the ordinary; (iii) that the moral values and behaviour encouraged by the family were reinforced by the school.

I think this school doesn't create a gap but my experience of mixed/state schools has led me to believe that they do create a gap. For example at home when being told off you are taught to lower your head but in mixed schools the teacher expects you to look at them when being talked to. (OTH)

I like this school because it is an Islamic school where I am accepted for my religious behaviour and I am provided with facilities to practice my religion without any care. (OTH)

I like school because it is friendly, homely and you feel welcomed. The advantages are it is all girls, it is a Muslim school, there are no boys so we don't have to keep our scarves on all the time. (OTH)

The Muslim girls in Old Town High did not reveal tension and confusion in their replies and this is similarly reflected in the interviews of both the Muslim and non-Muslim staff of this school. If there were concerns, they felt that they had ready resources in other Muslim members of staff or the headteacher with whom they could discuss such issues. They also felt comfortable that should any problems arise, the students were able to discuss them in their Islamic Studies lessons or assemblies.

> I feel comfortable about discussing these issues. Yes, yes I do because I don't see that it is against any of the ethos of the school to develop. I'm interested in skills of communication and I just try to enable the girls to develop their skills as best they can. Certainly in the texts that we do, we're looking at women who have challenged the establishment but not necessarily rebelled against it. I think there's a difference and I think this is why I like working here, because I do feel girls are taught here to fulfil themselves without necessarily rebelling against their own system and their culture but to see how to change things within the culture for the better. Hopefully, we give them an idea of all sides of the argument and I do think it happens here. (OTH)

Breakdown in communication is an important factor here and language becomes relevant. Many of the staff at City State voiced concern over the language needs of their students and the difficulties of communicating with their parents because of the language barrier. Of particular relevance to this chapter is the comment of one member of staff at City State, who felt that the language barrier was to some extent responsible for encouraging the Muslim students to group together while in school.

> I think one of the reasons that the girls like to stick together is that although they speak very good English there's still this language barrier because they'll say, 'Miss, I can't explain to you, I don't know the words to, to be able to tell you,' or 'Miss if I told you, you wouldn't understand'. There's this thing amongst them that they understand each other, obviously, but that we are not going to understand their little ways and we are not interested in their ways. I mean I'm fascinated and love to hear, but it takes a heck of a lot of encouragement to get them to tell you something about their background. I suppose therefore they stay together to protect that. (CS)

Several issues are raised here. It is notable that those areas of concern highlighted by the staff and students in City State are just those areas in

Old Town High where the staff and students feel secure and comfortable. This stems from: (i) being all Muslim girls and therefore feeling comfortable about being able to practice their religion, and to discuss cultural norms and constraints while feeling secure and not having to worry about what others might think; (ii) having a mixture of Muslim and non-Muslim members of staff, so that any felt lack of knowledge of culture could be discussed with them; (iii) an Islamic ethos which permeates the school and the curriculum; (iv) strong and informal links between the parents and the school which build up a relationship of trust.

The perceived clash of expectation between home and school and the complicity on behalf of the Muslim students in shielding their parents from their own performances and misdemeanours and the behaviour of their peers of which they know their parents will not approve, inevitably become factors which contribute to weak home school links. This is in contrast with Old Town High, where the links are both strong and informal and where the school is centred in the community from which it draws its students. Here concerns voiced in the mosque or on the street corner are passed back to the headteacher. The parents are quite confident to communicate over the phone or 'drop into' school and, most importantly, the students are quite happy for them to do so.

This research indicates that the staff of City State are unsure in their relationships with both their Muslim students and their parents. There are students from other ethnic groups as well as from the White population in the school. Many are from a different class background from the staff and some of them see their future in terms of marriage, children and possibly some form of low status employment. Here the staff appear to have no problems in subsuming the discourses of class and 'race' beneath the discourse of gender, in the interests of encouraging students to be self-determining individuals. And they feel comfortable doing so. However, because of their cultural assumptions about the Muslim students, their parents and the Muslim community, the discourses are assumed to conflict. Woman becomes Muslim woman.

Students who are not perceived to be committed to academic achievement, further education and a career, or who do not bring themselves to the attention of the staff, or who appear to have switched themselves off from school for many and varied reasons are the ones who fall by the wayside. In the case of the Muslim students who fall into these categories and who need encouragement to participate in lessons, stereotypical cultural assumptions are an additional factor. This results in a vicious circle.

> So they just stand back and the sad thing is that sometimes even the teachers themselves having this viewpoint doesn't encourage our Muslim girls to achieve their potential. They have low expectations as well, I feel. True, this is it, this is the danger and the thing is now it's come to the point where the child stops, has stopped believing in herself. (CS — one of the three South Asian members of staff)

Equality in Difference?

Both schools emphasised their agreements with the aims of feminism — particularly liberal and radical feminisms — in terms of the following: equal access to the curriculum, the questioning of gender stereotypes, enjoyment of working in a predominantly female environment, the employment of female staff as role models and the adoption of an approach which seeks to make the actual experiences of women more central to the education of the students.

There are, however, clear differences between the two schools in terms of the experiences of the Muslim students. The staff and students in Old Town High feel 'comfortable' to negotiate at least the discourses of 'race' and gender, because they don't perceive them to be oppositional and they have the confidence to move between these discourses as and when the moment requires it. This is in contrast to the staff of City State who appear to be immobilised by the number of the different concerns in their dealings with the Muslim students. At City State the teachers have to speak to an obviously disparate audience. They do so anyway in terms of the class, age, power differentials, sexual orientation and physical ability of their students. However, the fact that they believe they share a similar cultural experience as women renders such differences to be less relevant to their shared experience of being women. Stereotyped images of what it means to be a Muslim woman appears to have an additional relevance which 'gags' the shared discourse of being a woman.

This has repercussions for City State's Muslim students. Although they have the advantage of being and learning in a multicultural setting where there is a wider range of subject options, staff expertise, activities, equipment and resources, they are in effect marginalised.

The analysis of the empirical data in both schools reveals that the equal opportunities policies and practices on 'race' and gender, adopted in good faith by City State, have served to promote anxiety in the staff concerning their dealings with their Muslim students and their parents. This is then reflected in the confusion and tension expressed by their Muslim pupils, which also affects their behaviour in class, their attitudes to academic achievement and success and their expectations on leaving school. Although they were given opportunities to address these issues on a series of professional training days, some staff, particularly the more experienced ones, felt that all the INSET did was to retrace old ground in ways that failed to equip them with a working and in-depth knowledge of the needs of the Muslim students and their parents.

> I often think that when we have INSET days and we do racism awareness it is important for me to find out about the different ethnic groups, particularly the Muslim girls, because there are so many of them and that would be helpful. Far more helpful than trying to go over the same ground of racial awareness because we're still getting racism from the staff. There is no two ways about that. We don't have that knowledge of their backgrounds. It's very easy to moan about their parents again, and a lot of that does go on, even though we are supposed to be racially aware here, and are so compared to a lot of other schools. But still we don't bend the system to meet their needs at all. We're still plodding along in this very English old fashioned system. (CS)

I have already referred to the concern of 'Black' feminists over the 'invisibility' of 'Black' students engendered by teachers distinguishing between 'race' and gender and treating them as a duality. This is true for the Muslim students in City State, who appear to be less self-confident in their school environment than their counterparts in Old Town High.

Although City State offers more to its students in terms of equipment, resources, subject options and extra-curricular activities, the Muslim students are effectively as shut out from these as are their counterparts in Old Town High. However, in Old Town High, the lack of equipment, resources, subject options and extra-curricular activities is more than made up for by the value and experiences of sharing a common background and cause.

> I think that helps educationally in that they feel valued and if they feel valued then they will do their best to learn. There is an atmosphere of wanting to achieve and wanting to do well which is infectious, just as the opposite attitude that 'so what, it's all rubbish' is equally infectious. I think if the girls come out feeling self-confident, even if they haven't had all the equipment and resources, then they will do well. *They feel they can and no resources in the world can give that sort of attitude.* (OTH) (emphasis added)

Speaking of the relationship between Freire's work and the development of her work as feminist theorist and social critic, hooks says:

> Again, I want to assert that it was the intersection of Paulo's thought and the lived pedagogy of the many Black teachers of my girlhood (most of them women) who saw themselves as having a liberatory mission to educate us in a manner that would prepare us to effectively resist racism and White supremacy, that has had a profound impact on my thinking about the art and practice of teaching. And though those Black women did not openly advocate feminism (if they even knew the word) the very fact that they insisted on academic excellence and open critical thought for young Black females was an anti-sexist practice. (1993, p.150)

The learning environment of City State is multicultural and the staff are concerned to combat gender stereotypes while trying to serve the needs of many. On a practical level this often means that they try to serve the needs of the consensus. Girls who are not positioned as 'normal' are positioned as other than, and less than, 'normal'. They are seen as different from what is normal and preferable: as special. This is the case for the Muslim students at City State. On the other hand, although the Muslim girls in Old Town High are still seen as 'special' and 'other' by virtue of the fact that they have their own 'separate' school, the difference is that they all share this 'specialness' and 'otherness' within the confines of the educational discourse (and to a certain extent outside it); and this then filters through to other areas of their lives. In this environment it is 'normal' to be a Muslim girl and this fact is celebrated. This means that there is a wider range of discursive positions open to them than their counterparts in City State and they are enabled to take these up because they receive an education couched in their own values. At any given moment it is shared experience, shared knowledge and shared culture which is built on.

This is not, however, the case for the Muslim students in City State. In Old Town High the students feel comfortable and confident in their more monocultural setting and are therefore enabled to pursue explorations of what it means to be a Muslim woman operating within the Muslim community. In this environment being a Muslim woman is not an issue. Whereas the Muslim students of City State are marginalised because of the multicultural nature of the school, where the staff felt confident in their abilities to deal with the common issue of being female but not confident in their abilities to deal with the complexities of difference. This means that the Muslim students in City State are less confident about being a Muslim student in an environment where being a Muslim woman is an issue.

The Muslim students in each school are not homogeneous in terms of religious adherence, class, physical and mental ability and linguistic ability but they do share the experience of being Muslim women, who at present belong to a disempowered group in Britain. It is in Old Town High, where the Muslim students are comfortable in their difference and where there is the discursive flexibility available to them, that the processes of exploration and questioning and challenging from within an Islamic framework can begin. This means that they are then freed and encouraged to concentrate on their academic achievement, and this, as bell hooks (1993) argues, is an antisexist practice in itself.

This research suggests that, at the moment, the common emancipatory goal of all feminisms is more likely to be reached by the students of Old Town High than by the Muslim students of City State, because they feel more able and are better placed to challenge their positioning. It is the Muslim students of Old Town High who find it easier to be poststructural feminists, because in this school the ways of 'dancing' with the discourses of 'race' and gender are more readily available.

Notes

1. To ensure confidentiality and anonymity each school is protected by a pseudonym.

2. Quotes from the staff and students of City State are followed by the initials, CS, and those of the staff and students of Old Town High by the initials, OTH.

3. This is not to say that in less structured situations the Muslim girls in City State conformed to the stereotype of the shy, retiring, unassertive Muslim girl. They did not.

4. This is evidenced by the quantitative analysis of the imaginative story which was concerned to investigate the attitudes of the students to academic success. It is not possible to include this evidence in this chapter but it can be found in Haw, K.F. Educational Experiences of Muslim Girls in Contemporary Britain; Social and Political Dimensions, unpublished PhD thesis, University of Nottingham, 1995.

Chapter 4

A journey into the unknown: an ethnographic study of Asian children

Ghazala Bhatti

We all try to make sense of the world we inhabit and each of us goes about it in a different way. Any meaningful attempt to portray a semblance of reality is never an easy task, particularly if it is an ethnographic attempt to represent other people's realities. Many temptations in the shape of existing theories loom large when a lone researcher is facing the task of capturing the lived experience of others. The joy must be overwhelming when well-defined hypotheses lead to a theory which can adequately structure a kaleidoscope of myriad images into a recognisable picture. But what if such theories fail to incorporate all the contradictions from the field? What if one's obedient loyalty to one particular stance in effect means discarding difficult unexplainable data? Should one let go of all the hypotheses, the data or the theory? Should one abandon the idea of the journey altogether and start anew?

This chapter argues that in the course of exploratory ethnographic research it is important to respond imaginatively to new and challenging data even if that means losing sight of previously held theories. While collecting data for an ethnographic study,[1] I found myself facing the vexed questions set out above. I was interested in studying the home and school experiences of a group of children in their teens. Several researchers have highlighted the importance of studying the connection between these two worlds in children's lives.[2] Initially I had intended to carry out a cross-cultural study. I was particularly interested in exploring the ways in which their experiences at home and at school impact on the lives of boys and girls from different ethnic backgrounds and how the children make sense of such experiences. As I was interested in studying White, African-Caribbean and Asian[3] children, my choice of school was guided by the mixed ethnic composition of its pupils. My choice of secondary school children was affected by the assumption that, unlike younger children attending primary or middle schools, children of secondary school age were probably more likely to be self-aware, articulate and critical of the adults who were responsible for their schooling and for their education in general. I was aware that my own perceived ethnicity and gender, that of a Pakistani woman, were bound to affect the kind of data I would be able to collect. It would have been naive to have expected otherwise. As Hammersley has noted:

> We are a part of the social world we study ... This is not a matter of methodological commitment, it is an existential fact. (1983, p.15)

As all empirical researchers realise from time to time (see for example Griffin, 1987; Wolpe, 1988) experiences in the field can challenge one's previously held assumptions and beliefs. I had assumed that collecting data from a comprehensive school would not pose serious difficulties because I thought I knew something about how schools operated. I had taught in inner city, mixed, comprehensive secondary schools, albeit elsewhere in Britain. In the same way, I had assumed that I would definitely encounter difficulties in gaining access to African-Caribbean and White children's homes, unlike Asian homes. I even tried to rehearse my arguments to overcome these expected barriers. What actually occurred was the opposite. The school did not have basic straightforward data at hand; for instance it took me a very long time to find out the ethnic background and gender composition of the children at school because according to the school all children were 'treated in exactly the same way'.

I had not expected major difficulties over visiting Asian homes because I thought I could gain access culturally and linguistically to Pakistani, Bangladeshi and Indian homes. This indeed was the case. However, my anxieties about gaining access to African-Caribbean and White children's homes turned out to be unfounded. I was successful in befriending many children. As will become evident in this chapter, a conscious decision to respond to the data rather than try to control them in order to be coherent, structured the unpredictable course and outcome of my ethnographic journey.

What guided the final focus of the research on Asian children was the dearth of published material in the field of home and school based research, particularly with reference to working class Asian children. That, and the severe constraint of time. Contrary to my expectations, allowing my informants space to speak to me 'in their own voices' meant that I had to invest far more time than I could ever have planned in advance. This was because the field work was very slow. In order for me to respond to the data, the field work had to be carried out at the pace chosen by my informants. I was forced to slow down and walk in step with them. Had I rushed past them, the final yield in terms of data would not have been rich and intricate. The outcome of such a method is described in some detail later in this chapter. When I was about half way through my field work I realised that to do justice to African-Caribbean, Asian and White children, I would have to invest at least one more year on a full-time basis so that I could check my home-based research interpretations with the informants themselves. This did not include the additional time which was required to interview teachers and transcribe audiotapes. Neither did it take account of other unpredictable delays in the field. In the published research literature at that time there seemed to be anthropological (see Anwar, 1979; Werbner, 1990), political (Eade, 1989) and sociological (Robinson, 1986) studies of Asian communities in Britain. However, there seemed to be, in the late 1980s, an absence of critical discussion about the link between the findings from these studies and the present experiences of ordinary, working class Asian school children attending ordinary local education authority schools.

Putting aside the 'hard won' data negotiated over many days and months is a painful exercise. I had hoped that my reluctant focus on just Asian children and their parents' experiences, would have at least one positive consequence: a tighter focus on Asian communities would enable me to sketch a harmonious picture which could be neatly tied together into a logical sequence. Contrary to my expectations however, I ended up yet again with what appeared to be discordant data, with at least three sets of images from at least three very different sets of informants: the teachers, the parents and the children. Each of these, individually and collectively, told a totally different story and they adamantly refused to sing harmoniously together. Or was I failing consistently to tune into the right frequency?

The inevitable result of self-questioning and frequent reversals of expectations made me feel that I was losing control over the data. They seemed to be growing in unforeseen directions. This caused renewed self-doubt and yet another close scrutiny of the emerging data. Somewhere in the process of analysis, reflexivity and reanalysis, I let go of my obsession with discovering a single overriding theory. Perhaps it was not possible to find a model which takes account of structural forces in society and successfully link that to the micro-analysis of interaction in a small community, without dismissing new insights from the field. Losing control over the data meant in effect 'empowering' my informants. Allowing my informants to explain their own realities thus became one of the guiding principles of the study. The other was the analysis of the new data which were emerging from the field.

Methodological implications of the role of the researcher

Most of the data collected over a period of three years were based on lengthy interviews and conversations with 50 Asian families. I spoke to 50 Asian children, 49 Asian mothers and 24 Asian fathers. The sample included Hindu, Muslim and Sikh families who had migrated to Britain from India, Pakistan and Bangladesh. Many of the children had received their entire education in Britain. I also spoke to many of the 60, mostly White, teachers who were teaching at the school which the 50 children attended. These data were supplemented by participant observation and through detailed questionnaires in the case of teachers and children. The data generated were directly affected by the role I chose to adopt in the field as well as the role ascribed to me by my informants.

As far as the children were concerned, I was not their teacher. Neither was I their parent. In fact the children had not come across a researcher before. I was an unknown adult to begin with. Later on, I was befriended by many children and it was in the capacity of a friend that I visited them at home. Within children's homes I was not treated as an intruder. This is not to say I was not tested meticulously for trustworthiness. I had to 'earn' my entry to children's homes, including Asian homes. Children's comments during the latter part of research often demonstrated the ways in which I had been tested.

We had to make sure you were not a tell-tale. That's all. (Mala, 15 year old Indian girl)

Most Asian parents treated me as someone who knew their children at school and who could also talk to them at home in their own language. I was treated as the children's friend. I was never called by my first name but was assigned an honorary family relationship with reference to the speaker, such as Baji (sister). I was able to negotiate access more easily to mothers than to fathers. An Asian male researcher might have a different experience on account of his sex (see for example, Anwar, 1979). The ascription of a particular role inevitably leads to different, often contradictory, expectations from the researcher. I was dealing with three different sets of informants and they all perceived me in different ways. Due to lack of space it is not possible to elaborate on the different expectations my informants had of me.

I tried not to pass any moral judgements and I made a self-conscious effort to try not to let my preconceptions and bias affect the data. I sought to understand what my informants were trying to communicate to me rather than impose my own views upon them.

The teachers at the school I studied did not take my presence as a researcher very seriously. Generally speaking, they did not seem to hold academic research in high regard. This led me to believe that I was not seen as a threat by them. I was sent on errands by some male teachers. Some teachers expected me to help them in class. Although I did this whenever I could, I never assumed the role of the teacher and never stood in front of the whole class. I always sat with the children. Some teachers ignored my presence. This enabled me to observe them as well as the children. With the passage of time some teachers seemed to forget the purpose of my presence in school as I was increasingly seen as a voluntary helper of some sort. One teacher suggested that, perhaps, if I was lucky, I would be accepted on a teacher training course at the Open University. The ethical issues which emerged regularly from time to time were enormous.[4] I promised to keep the identities of people and places anonymous. All names have been changed to preserve confidentiality.

Making sense of the jigsaw puzzle

In this section I will draw upon some of the strands which emerged from the empirical data, which will help to explore at least three, broadly different views on related themes. Each view adds different dimensions of understandings and varying shades of subtle meanings to the initial picture. The following quotations and analyses have been chosen because they help to illustrate the usefulness of an open-minded enquiry. They help to tease out the intricate, unpredictable and often complicated pictures of others' lived realities. What follows is by no means a total picture of all the aspects of home-school relations in the lives of Asian children. That would require far more space than is possible here. The remaining section of this chapter merely constitutes some of the pieces of the jigsaw puzzle.

Asian parents and their views on schooling

I visited Asian parents at home to seek their views about their children's secondary school. The data reported take account of their 'own stories' as they shared with me their wider concerns beyond the issue of their children's schooling. These concerns included fears of unemployment, financial burdens in the case of several Asian, particularly Bangladeshi, families and the reasons for parents' migration to Britain. Only much later when they had developed trust in me, did they talk about their children's school. Thus the data reported below were embedded in a sea of other, more diverse data. It could not have been accessed immediately I visited the families. The background view which Asian parents presented helped to provide me with a meaningful context for analysing the following data.

Most of the Asian parents I spoke to held teachers in high regard, though these views changed when things went wrong. This attitude was related to parents' own experience of education. This in turn affected their expectations of their children's teachers. But even within the broad category of 'Asian parents', there were many views:

Just when after sending four children to school, I learnt that CSE is for Matric-fail types and O Levels is for the bright ones, they are going to make it all one. Why will they make it all one? [reference to the then new GCSEs about which leaflets in English were being sent home. This mother could not read English]. (Pakistani mother, translated from Urdu)

They write, they tell me, on bits of paper and then they hand it all in. No textbooks to cram from, just bits of paper. It is a mystery to me what my own child does in school every day ... I know very little about my son's work, yet he says he is doing OK; let's see. (Pakistani father, translated from Urdu)

For parents who did not go to school in Britain the education system was shrouded in complete mystery. The mother quoted above was referring to 'Matric', which is a basic school matriculation certificate in the Subcontinent. The use of the words 'Matric-fail' have a deep sense of shame attached to them. In this mother's past experience educational failure, in the sense of a candidate not passing a Matric exam, was frowned upon. There is both incomprehension and implied derision in the particular terminology she was using. In the second quote a father was trying to understand how his son's school operated. Fathers like him were very typical in their expressed interest in their children's schooling and in their lack of self-confidence when approaching the school on their own. Particularly poignant are the following examples from interviews of parents of the powerlessness which assails working class parents when they are facing what they perceive to be a powerful institution like a secondary school.

The following comments are typical of what the parents had to say. Two are by fathers and three from mothers. Asian parents are not alone in experiencing feelings of apprehension. Other working class parents probably experience similar feelings. What makes it still more difficult for Asian parents is the lack of facility in spoken English combined with inherent fear and hesitation built into the situation. They do not want teachers to feel sorry for them and at the same time they do not know how to proceed. As can be seen below, each parent gave a different reason but there was remarkable similarity in the feelings of inhibition displayed, together with complete powerlessness. The majority of Asian parents went into school on one or at most two occasions during their children's secondary school careers. I am quoting so many parents in order to illustrate the subtle variety of worries and concerns which the parents expressed.

> I went to my son's school once. They [teachers] were very polite when I got there but I will not go again. It smelt strange (embarrassed laughter) and I felt afraid. I should have taken my sister ... You see the children stare at you and you don't belong ... You are in a strange place. (Pakistani Mother, translated from Panjabi)

> Because I haven't been to school here I feel awkward, Baji [sister] ... and stupid. The teachers are so clever, so sure of themselves aren't they? You just feel silly. (Pakistani father, translated from Panjabi)

> You have to have a good reason. Your child goes because he has to learn good things. You go because ... well, you can't can you? You can't just go in for no reason and... just because you worry about him. (Bangladeshi father, translated from Sylhetti and broken Urdu)

> My daughter has forbidden me from going again. She feels ashamed of me you see ... It seems all her Pakistani friends in her year are the same. (Pakistani mother, translated from Panjabi, taped conversation)

> If I could speak good English it might be better, but I am so busy ... It is ten at night when I finish all the housework and my children don't want to teach me [English]. They are busy too. It's not easy. (Pakistani mother, translated from Urdu, taped conversation)

Within the context of the particular conversations from which these comments are taken, none of the parents had any specific complaints; they were sharing with me their general feeling of unease. It was difficult to know how far the teachers were aware of the particular situation facing Asian parents. It is also relevant that none of the teachers I spoke to spontaneously mentioned having seen Asian parents at school. Without extensive fieldwork in the children's homes, there was no way in which this aspect of home-school interaction would have surfaced. The usual comment I heard at school was simply that Asian parents did not come into school very often. The situation became very tense when a few of the parents did have particular complaints.

There is a scarcity of published research data in this very important area, and to the best of my knowledge, no one has as yet recorded such accounts of visits to schools by Asian parents. Every case uncovered may give us a clue about matters into which more systematic research is needed, within different schools and in different ethnic communities in Britain. It is not possible here to list the different anxieties which forced Asian parents to conquer their feelings of inadequacy and face the school for the sake of their children. There was one persistent parental worry however, that of truancy. I want to turn to this issue next.

A mother and a father, in two separate incidents, found their sons truanting and went to the school, in one case with the child, to discover what the teachers had to say about it. In the first case the boy was fourteen and in the second case fifteen. Both parents were dismayed that the school had not taken serious action or invited them in to discuss their son's difficulties. The mother who had discovered her son by chance in the shopping centre was shocked that his teacher had not realised he had been missing for over two hours.

> I know he wanted to learn Panjabi for a long time and the school can't teach that and I know he doesn't like French but that was no excuse. I nearly cried. I just took him back to school on the next bus and asked to see his form teacher. And, do you know something terrible, they did not even know he was missing! I was shocked, so shocked! They didn't care about him and he is only a child and he needs help. Can you imagine what I felt? (Indian mother, translated from Panjabi)

This mother was hoping the school would keep her informed and keep her son under a watchful eye. She was, in the end, dependent on her own relationship with her son to try to resolve the problem. Her son's school had gone down in her estimation because of this incident. She had never been to the school with a complaint before. There was, above all, a sense of betrayal and of having nowhere to go and no one to talk to about such matters. Apart from taking it up with the school she felt there was nowhere she could turn for professional advice. She told me that I was the only person to whom she had spoken about this so openly, other than her immediate family and the form teacher.

In another case, a father who came home unexpectedly one day to find his son at home was even more dismayed. He took a friend with him to visit the school because he was apprehensive about going alone.

> They made us sit for fifteen minutes in the corridor and then this lady wanted to know what the problem was. She said there was no problem with my son; that he could get a job somewhere. He is in fifth year. But I said I wanted him to study, and she said 'You worry too much Mr Khan'. I felt strange... All these years I thought they cared... And she never said he had missed school. I then thought it was a bad school but it was so iate. Couldn't... (silence)... couldn't do anything. (Pakistani father, translated from Urdu)

Both these parents told me they would not send their younger children to the same school. They were both to discover to their deep distress, after talking to their sons, that the boys were regular truants and had been truanting for some time. They felt deeply worried about other truants in school.

> They are children. They can get killed by a car or something and nobody will know where they are. Something must be terribly wrong with that school. I am going to tell my friends not to choose that school for their children. (Pakistani father, translated from Urdu)

His son did not get admission into the sixth form to re-take his exams and was very upset. At the point at which my fieldwork ended, he was trying to gain entrance to the local college of further education.

Teachers' views on schooling: 'Treating them all the same'

The immediate response, and the most common one, about children's ethnicity was that the school did not differentiate between people because of their ethnic backgrounds.

> Surely, to pick children on grounds of their colour is itself racist? No, why should one talk only of them and not of others? (Deputy head)

In nearly two years of field work in school, only three out of 60 teachers initiated the topic of Asian and African-Caribbean children. The frame of reference for the majority of the teachers was:

70

This is the kind of school we work in; we are all in the middle of a pudding at the moment [reference to the then new National Curriculum] ... We have to deal with several children, some of whom just happen to be Asian and West Indian. (Religious Education teacher)

The other predominant view was that:

Given our intake I reckon we are not doing too badly [academically]. We treat all children in exactly the same way here, though in terms of mixed ability, some topping and tailing goes on. (Maths teacher, field notes)

The speakers saw no problem with their view.

One day as I stood near the window in one of the classes with the head of CDT, we saw three Bangladeshi boys follow their teacher of Bengali out of another class. The head of CDT, who had been talking about the school in general, at that point turned around to look at me and said 'I think we are bending over backwards to accommodate some children'. Two Asian children sitting within earshot doing some assessed work, who followed our gaze outside the room, looked up at him for one split second and then at me. He seemed to believe that the school was already doing too much and should not do any more than it was already for the kinds of children who walked by outside.

In complete contrast, was another opinion to be found in the school. Judging by actual conversations I had with individual teachers, however, this was held by only a small minority; five White teachers in all spoke to me about it. They believed that the school was most certainly not doing enough for Asian children but that it was pretending to, so that Asian parents were not aware of the true picture.

I guess schools are like that. They only respond to pressure from vocal middle class people, and your average Asian parents are not that! (History teacher)

Children from African-Caribbean and Asian backgrounds were very seldom mentioned as a distinct category except by some who saw some Asian children as presenting the school with 'the language problem'. There was no indication, however slight, that African- Caribbean children had needs which were not being met.

Occasionally, in connection with Asian children, teachers volunteered explanations based on gender differentiation. Six teachers, all women, told me that in their opinion Asian boys on the whole seemed to have been brought up not to respect women and that they seemed to be more impressed by men. One of the explanations cited in conversation was that:

> Dad must go out to work and they see their mothers and sisters sitting at home not doing anything except housework and these mums can't control their sons always ... They don't know what's happening in the outside world.(Religious Education teacher)

When I asked how many such mothers she had actually met in person in connection with the children she taught, she said Asian parents never came into school anyway. In fact she had not met a single Asian mother. The majority view about Asian women that prevailed at school was that they did not go out to work and that the girls, too, would therefore not go out to work but would get married quickly or stay at home until they got married.

Several teachers, both male and female, told me they could not understand Asian children's repeated requests for extra tuition and that they talked...

> Ad nauseam about some kind of home teachers. I told them most teachers are school teachers and that those that aren't, can't be teachers. (English teacher)

The children were referring to the voluntary helpers in a local project, whom they called home teachers. The teacher was assuming that Asian children had some 'cultural problems'. The children in fact knew something this teacher did not know about home teachers.

Many teachers also believed that Asian families were all very united and they 'all help each other out don't they?'

> They are all interconnected in some way and boys can find jobs with cousins and relations. (PE teacher)

Some teachers mentioned that they were puzzled by the fact that Asian boys did not like going on work experience in a shop as a shop assistant and that they felt that somehow that was beneath them. The teachers felt that was rather an arrogant stance when 'our children (meaning White working class children) don't seem to mind it that much.' No distinction was drawn here between Bangladeshi, Pakistani and Indian children.

Asian children's views on life in school and beyond

Children could see the points of view of both their parents and their teachers and they tried to make sense of them. Girls saw things quite differently from boys. For example, marriage was not a recurrent feature in boys' conversations in the sense in which it was in girls'.

> Your teachers treat you as though you'll get married and have a dozen children, your mum and dad say they would like you to be educated ... and look what happens, you end up doing a silly job! (Bangladeshi girl)

This girl was working in a supermarket because she felt she had no choice. She was the oldest child and both her parents were unemployed. Boys were under pressure to improve on their fathers' track records. This was not always easy. Most Asian boys took their fathers' achievements as a starting point.

> He came here with £20. Look at him now, and all in 20 years! What can I do to do better for the family? (Pakistani boy)

None of the Asian boys I interviewed wanted to be shopkeepers, even those whose families had well-established businesses. They wanted to be engineers, or go into computing, or they displayed uncertainty about their future occupations. Some said they wanted to study further, rather than take over the shop. Many discussions with boys about future plans ended in bouts of grave uncertainty as they displayed diffidence and lack of self-confidence.

> My Dad thinks that if you study hard you are sorted out for life. What job can that be? Not a pilot or a scientist, oh no, only a shopkeeper. (Pakistani boy)

Another boy, who had just returned from visiting his extended family in Sheffield, said one day:

> My cousin-brother at the beginning was very upset about the shop and that...now he just accepts it. He has an HND. Didn't come in handy. (Pakistani boy)

It was explained to me that this cousin was better off running his family business than waiting to be employed after HND. He had not been offered a job despite making several applications. There were also boys in the sample who said they were never going to work in shops, no matter what.

> It's damn hard work, twelve hours a day at least, and a heart attack at the end of it! What's the point? (Pakistani boy)

This boy's father was a shop-owner and a heart patient.

At the same time, children of parents who were not educated were painfully aware of their parents' inadequacy and the school's inability to help them.

> I must help stock the shelves in the shop at night. You know yesterday I was there till ten because my Dad had a stroke in February and he can't lift things ... and then I went to sleep ... I couldn't hand in that assignment today and project work. (Pakistani boy)

> If I'm drawing that's fine but my mum doesn't know, she'll say things like - get this from upstairs when you have finished, or do you want a hot drink now? (Bangladeshi girl)

Even though Asian parents wanted their children to do well, they were not always able to help. On the whole, working class Asian parents trusted the teachers to do what was in the best interests of the children. Children knew this and used the information to suit themselves. This might also be true of many White parents and their children. This was certainly the case in most of the families in my sample.

> My Dad's too much in respect of teachers. He never says this to you [the researcher] but he is frightened of going into school, so there is no chance of him even seeing what school's really like! (laughter). (Maqbool, Bangladeshi boy)

Maqbool did not give letters and school invitations to his parents. According to him, they were not going to be 'understood' so he did not see the point in giving out letters. This practice was very widespread among both boys and girls. Some boys told me they tore up letters about school events and scattered them on the way home.

As far as teachers were concerned, children had definite views. Some of these views are expressed below. Children were very critical of the 'bad teachers' who did not have a sense of humour. Similarly, they were fond of others who talked to them as individuals. Some examples are quoted below.

> Well Mr McLaren you see. He is caring. He will always stop and ask how the lesson was and if things are OK at home, and he looks worried when I miss his lesson ... and he gives out notes to me and that is very kind. (Pakistani boy)

Children often sat and discussed what kind of human being had married or was going to marry a 'bad' teacher. Food always seemed to be important to children of this age.

> Maahin: She'd [the teacher] probably feed him spinach soup everyday.
>
> Shama: Yuck and cabbage and brussels sprout salan [curries]. Yuck yuck.
>
> Sohel: He [the teacher] will spend all his time looking grumpy. He'll never buy his wife a treat. He never gives us sweets not even [at] end of term.

Some children spoke explicitly about racist teachers, too, but there is insufficient space to dwell on this important topic here.

Conclusion

If we listen to all the informants, allowing them to clarify their meanings and explain their descriptions of their own realities, then we will gain some new insights from the field. If I had rushed to collect data and if I had not allowed my informants to share their slowly emerging views, I would have collected very different kind of data which would arguably not have been as receptive to the informants' 'own voices'. In this chapter I 'let the voices speak'. In the end, the main focus of exploratory ethnographic research must remain on the informants themselves. Without them it could not have taken place. If the experience of embarking on an exploratory journey means letting the informants steer the course of the journey, so be it.

Notes

1. Bhatti, G. (1994) *Asian Children at Home and at School:* An Ethnographic Study, Thesis submitted for the degree of Doctor of Philosophy at the Open University.

2. See for instance Tomlinson (1984) and Douglas (1964).

3. For the purpose of this article the term 'Asian' stands for those people whose parents originated in or migrated from India, Pakistan and Bangladesh.

4. Sometimes during the course of research, as in this instance, I let my informants hold an erroneous view about me. In this instance if I had stopped and corrected the teacher in mid-sentence it might have seriously affected the negotiation of further access. I felt at the time that if I was not seen as a threat I was more likely to obtain unguarded information.

Chapter 5

Reconceptualising Equal Opportunities in the 1990s:
a study of radical teacher culture in transition

Lynn Raphael Reed

Introduction

This chapter reports the findings of a small scale research project based on life histories from selected secondary teachers, in two large cities in southern England, who sustain a commitment to working with children in disadvantaged contexts. I believe that I have gained access to a more radical teacher culture than Mac an Ghaill has tackled (1988, 1990) and that this needs documenting and analysing, particularly in its aspects of transition. I am using the term 'radical' in a Freirean sense:

> The radical, committed to human liberation, does not become the prisoner of a 'circle of certainty' within which he (sic) also imprisons

reality. On the contrary, the more radical he is, the more fully he enters into reality so that, knowing it better, he can better transform it. He is not afraid to confront, to listen, to see the world unveiled. He is not afraid to meet the people or to enter into dialogue with them. (Freire, 1972, p.18)

Out of thematic and theorised analysis of the data, I have attempted to explore the situated pedagogical understandings of such teachers and to investigate their cultural reactions to the education policy directions of the late 1980s and 1990s. In part my intention has been to question how such teachers conceptualise the work that they do, and particularly how they articulate their commitment to equal opportunities. Equal opportunities is being used here as a term to encompass understandings of the complex interplay of issues around 'race', class, gender, sexuality, disability and special educational needs. This study was not focused on issues specific to 'race' and racism alone; however, recurrent themes are of significance to the debates around how to challenge racism and promote social justice in and through education. In conclusion, I attempt to elaborate a reframing of the discourse of equal opportunities, in keeping with the perspectives of these 'frontline teachers'.

Researching Teachers' Lives

There has, of course, been much written about teachers' lives, deploying three important strands of analysis identified by Cortazzi (1993). These are: analysing teachers' narratives from the perspectives of reflection, the nature of teachers' knowledge, and 'voice' and empowerment. It is not the purpose of this chapter to review this body of literature but it is notable that relatively little has been written in this genre specifically about teachers who work in disadvantaged contexts, or who have an explicit commitment to principles of social justice (Casey, 1994; Middleton, 1992; Weiler, 1988; Lee, 1984). This is despite the fact that many authors, who sustain the debate about equality and justice in education, conclude that the role of the teacher is critical, and that we need to know more about teachers' own perceptions and engagements with these issues:

Those who propose reforms often assume that by and large teachers are supportive of those reforms, and that they already have the appropriate inclination, background, commitment and ability to work towards the reforming agendas of democracy and equality. Their confidence is often misplaced. In my view, genuine reforms cannot be realised without an adequate theoretical understanding of the various ways in which teachers conceptualise their social world, and the ways these conceptualisations serve to define social relations of pedagogy and curriculum in schools. What is required is a systematic understanding of the nature of teachers' subjectivity and how it relates to the structural conditions within which schooling occurs, and within which teachers work. (Rizvi, 1994, p.213)

Such an understanding is what has been sought through this study. But there is also a second intention: to articulate the individual voices of these teachers, in part to challenge the control asserted over teachers' expertise, and to reveal the extent to which teachers remain powerfully articulate of their own understandings and practices. Far from revealing a secondary school culture where teachers fail pupils through holding 'unquestioning and ultimately irrational commitments' (Chief HMI Chris Woodhead, reported in the *Times Educational Supplement* January 27th, 1995), I have encountered teachers with a considerable depth of understanding about learning and who constantly question their practice in the search for improvement of pupil achievement.

The articulation of voice through the telling of a story is undoubtedly problematic and it is worth noting some dimensions for consideration. The means of production of the narrative has significance, including the relationship between researcher and researched, particularly in its aspects of power (Roberts, 1981; Ball, 1985). Language itself fundamentally affects that which we can know through the process of life history research:

There is no clear window into the inner life of a person, for any window is always filtered through the glaze of language, signs and the process of signification. (Denzin, 1989, p.14)

That which counts as knowledge to be shared is itself socially constructed and reflects unequal access to rightful voice (Anderson et. al., 1990). These concerns fundamentally open up the nature of research to the reflexive exploration of the critical researcher (Hammersley and Atkinson, 1983), and challenge the notion that research evidence must be 'objective' and singular in its status. Not only is the participants' evidence seen as narrative, but the research process may be read as fiction:

> Fields like history, anthropology, sociology and political science, fields that depend upon interpretation and imagination, are themselves literally fictions-things made (Geertz, 1973). They are the results of a framework-defined world transacting with a framework-dependent mind. The facts never speak for themselves. What they say depends upon the questions we ask ... What we believe, in the end, is what we ourselves create. (Eisner, 1993, p.54)

From this perspective, all research is a form of storytelling. This has lead me to engage in extensive, conversational, unstructured interviews with these teachers, some of whom I know very well indeed. In terms of a research relationship, not just a teacher/learner relationship, this proposes a dialogical interaction between researcher and researched that overcomes subject-object dualism; where the process of research itself becomes transformative (Gitlin et. al., 1993). It also acknowledges that 'genealogies of context' (Goodson 1992) may be shared, and that teachers, like pupils or indeed researchers, are active subjects within their lived experience.

Frontline Voices: teacher testimony as evidence

The fourteen teachers who have contributed to this study constitute a network sample. A number of them are known to me in different settings as practitioners, and whilst they have a variety of teacher styles, they all share the reputation, supported by evidence from pupils and other staff, of being effective in role. This initial core suggested names of other teachers who might be involved in the project. Not all of the participants are practising school teachers at present, though they all retain a working link with education, work in inner-city contexts and sustain a commitment to challenging inequality. The sample includes: a registered OFSTED inspector (GN); a secondary Head (SP); two Deputy Heads (ST and DE); a pastoral senior teacher (OC); a sixth form centre curriculum area leader (BW); a teacher educator (BD); a peripatetic literacy worker (CS); the team leader of a project for raising the achievement of African-Caribbean pupils (NW); a teacher supporting excluded pupils and pupils at risk of exclusion (PK); a senior teacher in an MLD school (DS); a head of

Humanities (MS); an inner-city drama teacher (SD) and a vocational curriculum coordinator (RV). Half of the sample is female. The ethnic composition reflects the distribution of teachers by ethnicity in the wider population; that is, the majority of the sample are White.

What is striking about these transcripts is the eloquence and intelligence in their articulation. It will come as no surprise to hear that all of these teachers have pursued vigorous, continuous professional development, many achieving higher degrees en route. A number of them received their initial training in innovative initial teacher education programmes employing principles of reflective pedagogy and extended professionalism.

As with all such projects, there is a considerable quantity of material gathered, but for the purposes of this chapter I wish to identify just two sets of recurrent themes.

Emancipatory Teaching and Learning

These teachers demonstrate a clear sense of the significance of the social construction of identity, with the process of teaching in challenging contexts being about the testing of the self and the strengthening of one's own identity (Reed and Beveridge, 1993):

> Constantly that work was making me define to myself more clearly — who I was, what I believed in and why. Having to articulate what I believed to other people who didn't come from the same position as me at all and having to argue things out and work things out in a context together, no matter how mucky, was a real challenge, in a way that I didn't expect. The philanthropic part was about the challenge to make 'them' homogeneous with what my expectations were, but in the event, the challenge was much more about the deconstruction of myself, the questioning of myself through other cultural positions — not for any of us to become the other, but to clarify where we stood and why. (MS)

and

> I think I have come across teachers who are frightened of situations and frightened of teaching and frightened of children. I have come across an awful lot more teachers who are frightened of themselves.

Being a teacher in these circumstances not only asks you to confirm your own identity, but it requires you to acknowledge who you are to the pupils as well, which very few teachers feel capable of risking. (DS)

The process of teaching as an act of becoming is mirrored by a vision of learning as a creative act:

The whole process of becoming a teacher for me was about adding layer after layer to a belief about the importance of interpersonal things, that all this stuff in books about the curriculum is really a red herring, because what is actually important about being human is not accumulated knowledge, but being interactive — how you are with other people ... The high note has been those moments where the humanity of these young people as evidenced by things that they've done, is overwhelming: quite tear-jerking ... The process of teaching ... is about touching the creative part in all of us. (RV)

And again:

I love the moments of almost breathless... holding the breath, when somebody in the class says something or reads something that makes them pause and they become aware, and the class becomes aware, that this is a whole new area of that person. Both teaching and learning in that sense become part of identity formation situated in specific historical and cultural contexts. (CS)

To have an idea of where they're going is very important, both individually and collectively. And to know where you're going, you have to know where you've come from. (NW)

This conception of teaching and learning involves the opening up of a dialogic relationship in the classroom, where the shared construction of understanding in the act of learning is made central (Shor and Freire, 1987). Cultural dissonance which strains the social relations of the class-room — including the discourses of racism, sexism, and homophobia as they inhabit the classroom — is seen as problematic to these teachers. A key feature of intervention to challenge inequalities is then represented as getting involved in those classroom discourses:

I remember one of the first classes I had was a fifth year CSE class ... The dynamic of their relationships was incredibly powerful — what was going on between them, and between them and the outside world was the context really for an awful lot else. 'Runnings' for example could structure almost every interaction, even when you tried to suppress it and might appear as the teacher to be in control. The way in which kids ran each other down using the language of racism, sexism, homophobia etc. and the whole set of conventions around the words, the terms, the meaning of the terms, the looks, the body posture, who it was who became the object of certain 'runnings' and how the parrying of those would in itself demonstrate a certain kind of power — all formed part of a very powerful game that constructed the relations in the classroom. I felt really ignorant of what those social processes were about but also that I had to find some way to bring my cultural understanding into play with their cultural understanding. I mean, about 'runnings', I had a kind of moral position about it. When I looked at the effects upon these boys — the way in which certain boys had low status, the way they were made to feel insecure by that process, the amount of damage that was done. And this included the damage to the boys who were successful at it, as it boosted their sense of power and manipulation of power in a way that didn't seem that healthy. (MS)

Engagement for these teachers in this social context for learning is not always easy. They experience tensions in dealing with the sometimes conflictual dimensions of 'race' and gender:

There are the tensions between issues of gender and ethnicity which often feel difficult to handle. Sometimes I feel the need to resist or challenge antagonism not from a position of White authority but from a position of feminist outrage, you know, 'How dare you treat me like shit. You say to me that you feel like you're being treated like shit, stop treating me the same!' I've found ways of bringing that out. I don't think that I do it very well, but I try to make it part of the explicit agenda — which is to talk about power, and to point out how different people in different ways in social relations in the world become the objects of power-players in a game of power that structures relationships unequally in the world, and that people carry that within them and between them in ways that reproduce inequality and reproduce hurt. They are showing in school their emotional reactions to the abuses of power, but so am I and I feel that they need to see that. There is lots of bad language between them, often to do with mothers, and particularly around sexuality, and I let them know how that makes me feel as a woman and a mother. I bring my gendered self into the arena and I think it's important that they see that. (MS)

Again and again the emotional aspect of this relationship is identified, where the impact of pupil behaviour on other people at an emotional level is stressed as a vital part of the learning frame:

I basically believe in positive anger. I think that kids have a right to see others angry and hurt by their actions. ...A loving anger that brings all kinds of issues into play. (OC)

and

My argument is that with most of the children I can work with them to some degree if I am allowed to maintain the boundaries that I set for them ... If that is taken away then what you are basically saying is that you are going to suspend vast amounts of children. I know this leads us into muddy waters, but to me it is just commonsense. You have to respond. You have to engage with these difficult behaviours with a degree of respect for the child. I also think that it is healthy to show your anger to a child — I mean to show them that they have gone beyond the bounds of acceptable behaviour and that that produces a response. (DS)

There are of course tensions between holding, through authority, the clear boundary frame of the classroom, and sharing of power over the act of learning (Crozier, 1994). This is acknowledged as an area of potential conflict that the teacher may not be able to resolve, but which can be made conscious:

What it requires that is very difficult is a belief in your right to ask difficult questions, to raise those painful and difficult issues around conflict and dis-ease, and then be prepared to hear the answers... It means you have to look honestly at what was going on in the social space of the classroom, and in a sense engage with your fears and failures as a teacher. I think as a teacher I often can't let go enough to

84

really hear pupils in these areas, so that real debate, real discussion, real truth-telling and some sense of transformation doesn't happen that often in my classroom. I want to direct things too much. (MS)

All these teachers have had experience of developing antiracist and antisexist curricula, and many were involved in the creation of explicit schemes of work with a radical bias. What is interesting here is the manner in which they reflect a growing re-evaluation of some of those ways of thinking about an equal opportunities curriculum:

> When I came to the school there was this very radical and antiracist and antisexist Humanities Curriculum which looked on paper as if it had the potential to transform through explanation all kinds of under-standings about inequality. But what I felt increasingly strongly was that embedded in this emancipatory curriculum was still a patronising sense of control. Teaching about the history of slavery, for example, still placed Black pupils as the objects of history — not empowered to construct their own, relevant, lived agenda. It also, in a perverse way, sustained a victimised account of identity, and easily fed student opposition. Eventually I wouldn't teach about Black History in that way, and certainly not about the history of slavery.

> What I came round to feeling was that emancipatory teaching was about giving pupils the means to understand better where they were coming from and to give them the means to be critical about what influences them. It is about being able to articulate themselves, to become themselves more clearly, not enforced into categories by the constructs of others, not constructed in another person's image - whether that be other pupils in the room or me, the teacher, with my 'right on' curriculum. (MS)

This doesn't mean that these teachers have stopped drawing political issues explicitly into the taught curriculum. This often focuses on identification of a common cause:

> You can see the mentality that exists, that you can feel good if there is somebody lower than you that you can look down on. But that's not the only model for organising a society, and it's not the only model for organising the education system. Of course there are hierarchies, and the conflicts that exist are conflicts about keeping people in their

place. But there is another way with children to take this on in a real sense through identification. No two people experience oppression in the same way but they may experience oppression and how it feels to feel downtrodden. If you understand those things, then you can shout out — you can say 'No, this isn't right'. You have to have a vision of transformation to pass that on, and help them to find new ways of making sense of the world. (NW)

Specific examples of this were given by a number of people:

The best example I can describe to you is working with a group of boys in drama on pregnancy and termination. (SD)

This teacher wrote about this at length in an assignment for her M.A.

It is important in this work to go deep. Towards the end of the afternoon they are deep in role. One 'mother' will not accept that her unborn child may be born with cerebral palsy. She is supported sympathetically by her 'husband', though he confides he is in despair. She, in addressing the 'doctors' who have recommended a termination, makes a powerful speech for her right to have a child. We are all moved. (SD)

Another 'mother' doesn't want her child. She is already fractious with a second 'husband' who does not accept her older child by her first marriage. She attacks him for putting pressure on her not to terminate and accuses him of 'merely wanting the proof of his own virility'.

The lesson could have gone deeper and deeper — but time is always a factor. As we sum up and evaluate together at the end of the lesson, they comment both in and out of role. What emerges is the isolation many of the 'women' felt coping with lack of tolerance and understanding from male doctors and pressure from social workers. Many of the 'men' did not like their feeling of powerlessness, or felt inadequate in knowing how to support, or resentful that attention had been taken away from them. All agreed it was hard to make a decision. Listening to them going out I understood that they had been moved, but I also watched as their bodies shifted into their roles as being boys in an East End school ... shoulders reaching into the space to fill the corridors. (SD)

An education for social justice is in this way being pursued by these teachers, through the influence of productive social and personal relationships between pupils and teacher, combined with developing perspectives that encompass shared critical understandings of oppression across the fractures of 'race', class and gender. One of the Black teachers in this study identified this clearly:

NW: The antiracist practice of today is still about realising the experience of the past, how it affects us today and how we can still struggle to improve things, but that it is not only one group in struggle; it's all of us in struggle.

LRR: Does this raise particular issues about doing antiracist work with White pupils?

NW: Yes ... it's difficult. On the one hand they have to understand how they themselves can be oppressive to others through what they say and what they do, but at the same time they have to know that it's not their fault; that this is because they live in a certain society at a certain time.

Some White kids want to know more about you as a Black teacher and therefore, at the same time, also perhaps understand themselves more. If they want to do well then they've got to understand their teacher and they've got to understand what their teacher thinks ... There are certain kinds of tools that you can give them and that is for them not to go away with guilt, but to go away feeling that they have a contribution to make in changing things, and that they themselves are also oppressed and need that change to happen.

Embedded in these accounts, when they were asked to describe what was at the heart of the teacherly act, these teachers represented social constructivist theories of learning, even if not explicitly identified as such:

Increasingly I became effective as a teacher through dealing with some of the issues in the immediate social context, but also by sitting down with kids, paying real attention to their individual needs, and helping them by connecting with them in their world of meanings and taking their power over their own learning further forward. And the biggest, toughest kids, when you sit down with them like this, reveal a huge hunger for learning and a huge need to have that hunger met, with respect and dignity. (MS)

This includes awareness of the need for metacognitive strategies:

All children need someone to mediate their learning, but sometimes this feels especially true for children with special educational needs. For most of the pupils I work with who have moderate learning difficulties, they just don't pick things up in passing in the same way. It can help to help them to think consciously about how they do something. When I'm reading with children I ask them to tell me what they are going to do next — you know, 'I'm going to look along to the end of the sentence and see if that will help me to guess what that word is'. It's a standard predictive strategy that a reader uses without necessarily making it conscious like that. (DS)

These features of emancipatory teaching and learning perspectives, described with reference to actual classroom experience, help us in the important task of 'filling out' the theoretical perspectives articulated in radical academic texts. It makes us realise that the imperative to develop dialogic and transformative teaching, even in an increasingly bureaucratised and centralised education service, is possible to achieve. These particular teachers, unlike the teachers in Crozier's study, are willing to make themselves vulnerable and to constantly problematise the processes of teaching and learning, particularly in relation to controversial and political issues. They would agree that:

In order that the pupils can engage in such discussions they need to be provided with analytical skills; with the confidence to articulate painful experiences and/or to expose themselves to criticism from their peers. It also means breaking through prior experiences they have had of learning: breaking with old secure habits; changing their expectations; helping them not to feel insecure to which learning through a critical, analytical experience gives rise.

In order to achieve this, it would mean for the teacher, too, to 'break with old secure habits' and possibly to put themselves in a vulnerable position. (Crozier 1994, p.221)

Access and Achievement

A second recurrent feature in these teachers' accounts revolves around their attempts to deal with issues of access and achievement in light of wider policies:

> Of course with a falling roll we end up getting kids referred to us who have already been suspended from other schools or who have got into difficulty and they end up coming into a school that has already got more pressing needs than it can really deal with. Then there is what we call 'the snowdrift effect' — you know, those White middle class parents who might have sent their children here, able to work the system sufficiently that they get their kids into the school up the hill. White flight. (DE)

Many of these teachers expressed the feeling that policies on funding and on enrolment, special needs allowances and league tables created a tendency for schools to want to ditch their 'problem' students:

> Nobody has time any more or energy to deal with these pupils' needs. In all kinds of ways they are seen as too costly. The Special Needs review coming up is not going to make that any easier because a school like ours is bound to lose funds. (ST)

Having said that, there is an explicit commitment being struggled for to resist the tendencies to see such students as liabilities, and to insist on literal access to schooling for all:

> We've virtually reached a position of non-exclusion in the school which is quite controversial. I think exclusion gives a message about learning, that is, 'O.K. ... you've done wrong, and that's it. You're not going to be our problem so get out of the way'. Now I argue that it is part of learning about responsibility and taking responsibility to say, 'This is the problem, and you can't run away from it.' ... My feeling is that once you reach the point of exclusion you are pretty well ending that child's chance of educational success, and that concerns me. It also concerns me that all seventeen exclusions last year were of Afro-Caribbean pupils; fifteen of them were boys, and of the permanent exclusions, four were Afro-Caribbean boys and one was an Afro-Caribbean girl. I won't however make this public as a policy statement of the school. We are not yet ready for that. (SP)

In part, these moves are also seen as a response to parental pressure from an increasingly vocal and politicised section of the community. The strategy, though seen as politically right, is also seen as problematic:

> The Head is under a lot of pressure. There was a meeting about non-exclusion policies last term, a very angry meeting with a large audience demanding non-exclusion policies within the school, and demanding that Black youngsters are not discriminated against in terms of sanctions. But this is really hard ... It is a high risk strategy. If it works it will be good but it also creates a lot of instability when staff don't feel it's the right way or don't know how to make it work. I've seen staff set out to lay traps for kids. The world out there also remains hostile. Kids are going to places where people are still shouting at them and still giving them aggravation. If school seems real tolerant then the possibility is there for them to increase their 'acting out' behaviours 'cos they're not particularly worried about getting caught. (OC)

One teacher working specifically with pupils at risk of exclusion described graphically the feeling that certain school cultures marginalised pupils in need of specific support and teachers attempting to challenge that:

> PK: I think it is probably the most depressing time to be involved in trying to work with young people. I feel as if I am on a highway to nothing, trying to support young people who are also on a highway to nothing.

> LRR: What sort of things happen that make you feel that?

> PK: Oh God, just loads of things. Like not being given a room to work in when I go into school, or being given a room that is not suitable for the work I do so that pupils can feel safe in it. And having to fight with teachers all the time as to whether they will let a kid come out of class or not. If they're a kid in difficulty, but who is quiet and passive, then teachers are really hostile to that pupil missing 'real' lessons. But if they're a pain in the arse then teachers are quite happy to let them out of class. Then there are the totally unreal expectations of what you

can do with a young person. It's as if they think that you can just go in and turn them around, but you can't undo fourteen years' worth of damage in a few sessions.

This feels like a real equal opportunities issue to me. You know, pupils who have a specific learning difficulty are often seen as children to be sorry for, but a child with an emotional or behavioural difficulty is just seen as bad. And there are a number of pupils I'm working with at the moment whose needs remain completely invisible; White middle class girls who are well fucked up and need help. Pupils just seem to have become like commodities and no-one wants obviously damaged 'goods'.

Finally, I want to point up the permeation of the discourse of 'raising achievement' throughout the accounts. This seems to represent a response to a dominant current discourse in education about 'standards' and accountability:

If the school improvement movement can be characterised simply, then its main characteristics are to do with professional development and culture and ethos and relationships — all that liberal side of things. School effectiveness is characterised by measurement and numbers. In the best of both worlds, and I think you can have both, there is the possibility of reclaiming some of those good things that I experienced in the autonomous days of the 1960s and 70s; but placing that alongside more rigour — to make it part of the same framework. I don't think we've got to the stage where we can talk about this with ease because we've had such a battering from accountability along nonsense lines like crude league tables. This makes it hard to enter the target setting and accountability culture and hang on to the other goodness, but I think it would serve our purpose if we did. (GN)

I prefer now to talk about 'raising achievement' rather than 'equal opportunities'; in other words, 'equal opportunities with outcome'. (NW)

For some this had entailed a self-critical re-evaluation of the overtly politicised curriculum agenda of the radical left over the last two decades:

91

The agenda for me is now about rights of access; access to the analytical and conceptual tools to make sense of the world and not be treated as fodder for the revolution. That became more clearly articulated by the Black parents, teachers and governors' group, saying, 'Why don't you, the White liberal establishment who think that you've got a radical agenda through your antiracist curriculum, why don't you just take your hands off our children? Why don't you just let our children have access to the same kind of educational quality that White middle class children have as a right and that our children should have as a right, including good academic qualifications so that they have access to certain choices in life?' (MS)

This is paralleled increasingly by the issues of literal access to schooling — the right not to be excluded or suspended. Issues around an emancipatory approach to teaching and learning, as characterised earlier, then become critical:

So that's really what equal opportunities is. It's about ensuring things like equality of access, equality of provision and so on, but knowing that they are only possible through understanding the interface between these goals and the need to understand the child and their social and cultural world. (NW)

One point of significance to raise here is the fact that whilst this project was presented to all the teachers involved as being concerned with issues of 'race', class, gender, sexuality, disability and special educational needs, there was a tremendous amount of attention paid in their accounts to issues of ethnicity and the position of boys and working class male youth. Gender, from the point of view of girls, seems to have almost slipped off the agenda. It may be that this reflects the wider context of concern to have demonstrable markers of success in school interventions through the currency of credit accumulation. As Riddell notes:

Unless this wider social context is taken into account, the conclusion from girls' examination performance could suggest there is really no problem. (1992, p.46)

At the same time it highlights the necessity for a new research agenda which investigates further the significance of masculinity, ethnicity and schooling (Mac an Ghaill, 1994; Raphael Reed, 1995).

92

Reframing the Discourse of Equal Opportunities

What these teachers appear to be doing is bringing together in practice an embedded understanding of the issues raised by social constructivist psychology and a symbolic interactionist sociology, in a way that allows greater sense to be made of the learning process (Pollard, 1990). Within this they identify the importance of both cognitive and affective learning (Epstein, 1993) and also that:

> ... Education requires us to go beyond the conventional view of metacognitive knowledge as merely to do with cognitive or intellectual aspects of the learning process ... If autonomy in learning also depends on the establishment of democratic interdependence between persons in learning environments, then it is necessary to develop an understanding of social processes which constrain or enhance the construction of such interdependence. (Quicke and Winter, 1994, p.431)

Importantly, this conception is combined with an understanding of cultural positioning and multiple discourses of power, particularly relating this to the construction of identity. This is where the equal opportunities perspective, articulated by these teachers, begins to shift from an essentialist and reductionist view of 'difference' with rationalist beliefs about the translation of policies into practices, and to break from 'realist' conceptions of the curriculum. To quote Rattansi in his critique of 'some of the main underlying oversimplifications which have informed educational practices in the field of 'race' and education':

> ... We do ourselves no service if we neglect to ask fundamental, difficult questions about our understanding of some of the key issues, processes and terms involved; if we ignore contradictions in our underlying discourses; if we fail to grapple with the limitations of our assumptions about pedagogy and how subjects and subjectivities are formed; and if we fail to notice how economic, political and cultural differentiations are undermining older fixities around the ethnic, class and political identities of the minority communities. (1992, p.41)

These are the challenges which the teachers in this study are clearly working with.

93

It may be relevant that hardly any mention has been made by these teachers of present engagement with wider political struggle as educational activists. Perhaps this is a sign of our times. The external context has impinged on their perspective to the extent that accountability, access and achievement are now terms regularly used, signifying an attempt to construct a 'new' democratic agenda refocused on the community and demonstrable outcomes. The difficulties in working with 'community', defined within a radical agenda are highlighted by the tensions referred to over pupil exclusion and curriculum control.

This mirrors a growing debate within the Left over the future direction of education policy, where the advancement of an alternative policy position within a radical left or socialist agenda has been problematic (Rattansi and Reeder, 1992). Some are claiming a new, locally focused, democratic agenda based on community ownership and accountability rather than a return to LEA control (Atkinson, 1994; Arnot, 1991). Exemplars of such practices from North America, as well as New Zealand, Australia, the Netherlands and Belgium, are relatively well-developed (Marshall, 1994; Davies and Anderson, 1992).

Viewing social policy as discourse, we should also note certain shifts in the public representations of education and equal opportunities. The radical right has successfully attacked the egalitarian left, pillorying its concerns with equity and social justice as risible 'political correctness':

> In times of economic downturn, it has been relatively easy for conservative movements across the globe to mobilise a popular backlash against equal opportunity and civil rights initiatives. In a cultural era dominated by distrust, disillusionment and despair, the idea of public education has itself lost some credibility. (Rizvi 1994, p.203)

From within the Left itself, there has been a concern to re-examine the monolithism of key concepts such as multiculturalism and antiracism: to ask probing questions that take us beyond a critique of radical credentials (May 1994). Instead we have emerging an identity politics, which rejects the theoretical imposition of *a priori* socialist analysis, in favour of a perspective that seeks to empower the subjects of history through articulation and elaboration of rightful 'space' in the world of created meanings. In educational circles, this means looking closely and critically at the school context within which diverse and liberatory identities for pupils may, or may not, be engaged with. Unlike the earlier liberal agenda of cultural pluralism, this perspective acknowledges the significance of power, understands the role that schools can play in the reproduction of inequality and challenges unequal access to educational opportunity and achievement:

> ... Regardless of how well-meaning, educational institutions cannot move from 'soft' definitions of multiculturalism to more sophisticated ones without an understanding of the role the educational institution plays in the identity struggles of its students. The interface of dominant institutional norms and the struggle of students to form an identity constitutes a micro-political struggle, which takes place under the noses, but outside the consciousness, of most educational institutions. In addition ... when various voices within the students are not legitimated by the larger institution, even the students themselves lose access to those parts of themselves that might challenge institutional assumptions and explanations, thereby effectively 'silencing' themselves. (Anderson and Herr 1994, p.58).

It is of significance that the teachers in this study, working through praxis towards a rearticulation of their radical values, have projected perspectives so consonant with debates found in the wider literature. In any future reframing of policy for the pursuit of egalitarian ends in education, such cultural shifts by teachers committed to that goal will have to be taken into account.

Chapter 6

Racism and children's cultures

Richard Hatcher

'Race' in the cultures of White children is a relatively undeveloped area of research. In general, studies of children and 'race' have divorced 'race' from culture. Research from a psychological perspective into racial prejudice among children (e.g. Milner, 1983; Davey, 1983; Aboud, 1988) relies largely on experimental rather than ethnographic data. Evidence emerged during the 1980s of the extent of racial harassment in schools, from personal accounts (e.g. CRE, 1988), and quantitative research (Kelly, 1988; Cohn, 1988). While important in placing the issue of racism among White children on the agenda, these studies (with the important exception of the Burnage Report — Macdonald et al, 1989) shed little light on the situations in which it occurred, its functions, meanings, causes and consequences — in other words, on the place of 'race' within the cultures of White children. Yet if we are to tackle racism among children effectively it is precisely those issues which need to be examined.

Before discussing my own research, I want briefly to outline my perspective on racism. Firstly, racism has a situational specificity. Stuart

olating a common and universal structure to
ntially the same, outside of its specific histori-
It follows that 'Onc must start, then, from the
which racism accomplishes under specific
38). Hall is speaking of 'race' at the level of
remarks apply equally to the study of 'race' in
ty: in this case the work it accomplishes within
the cultures of children.

I take a second point from Hall: his emphasis on how racism must, 'to become a real and historical political force, connect with the lived experiences of the 'silent majorities" (Hall et al, 1978, p.30). Again, in the context of childhood, his remark directs our attention to the part that 'race' plays in the lived experiences of children.

Thirdly, I share Robert Miles' rejection of the idea that racism is an ideology that simply imprints itself on passive subjects. 'Ideologies are never only received but are also constructed and reconstructed by people responding to their material and cultural circumstances in order to comprehend, represent and act in relation to those circumstances' (1989, p.132). For Miles, racism is both a behavioural ideology and a cognitive ideology. It provides a rationale and motivation for social action as well as a framework for interpretation:

> racism may take the form of a relatively coherent theory, exhibiting a logical structure and adducing evidence in its support, but it also appears in the form of a less coherent assembly of stereotypes, images, attributions, and explanations which are constructed and employed to negotiate everyday life (1989, p.79).

Fourthly, as Miles insists, racism cannot be understood in isolation from other social processes: 'it should always be remembered that those who articulate it and those who are its object are located in a wider, complex web of social relations' (1989, p.133). The task is to identify what are the most salient social relations in children's cultures, and how 'race' relates to them.

It follows from this perspective on 'race' that the study of 'race' in children's lives needs to be situated in an analysis of its context — the cultures of children.

Children's cultures

There is a large body of work by psychologists on children's peer relationships (see Erwin, 1993 and McGurk, 1992 for recent overviews). Though they themselves acknowledge that there are many aspects of children's cultures that are not well understood, a great deal of light has been shed on the characteristics and functions of friendship among children, and the extent and significance of conflict in their peer relations (e.g. Asher and Gottman, 1981; Shantz and Hartup, 1992; Hart, 1993).

In contrast to the body of work that has been produced by psychologists, the sociology of children's cultures is relatively undeveloped (Chisholm, 1990). Nevertheless, there are several strands of sociological research which have addressed aspects of children's cultures. There is a small number of ethnographic studies of childhood itself (e.g. Sluckin, 1981; Davies, 1982; Fine, 1987). There is a rich body of work on 'pupil cultures' (e.g. Pollard, 1985; Woods, 1980), though its focus is largely restricted to the the child in its pupil role, and much of it deals with the secondary school. There are a few studies of gender relations among primary age children (Clarricoates, 1987; Thorne, 1993). Studies of relationships between White and Black children have tended to focus on the extent of inter-ethnic friendship (Denscombe, 1983; Denscombe et al 1986): Wright's (1992) study of racism among primary school children is an exception.

Davies' (1982) definition of the culture of childhood provides a useful starting point:

> Even without the rights enjoyed by adults, and despite the expectations placed on them as members of the institution of childhood, children busily get on with the business of constructing their own reality with each other, as well as making sense of and developing strategies to cope with the adult world as and when it impinges on their world. This reality and its related strategies I refer to as the culture of childhood. (p.33)

The strength of this perspective is its emphasis on the social constructivist nature of children's cultures. Its limitation, which derives from the symbolic interactionist framework it adopts, is its inadequate theorisation of the relationship between the micro and the macro, the world of children and the adult society. Children are active makers of social reality, but they do so in ways that are powerfully shaped by the adult society, both directly, through the family and the school, and indirectly, mediated by the social and cognitive processes of children's cultures.

The theoretical task facing sociologists of children's culture is posed well by Chisholm (1990). She is speaking of youth, but her remarks apply equally to children:

> Agency and hegemony are linked together in an image of the active subject in constant struggle with structured and structuring contradictions; the struggles result in dynamic but systematic patterns of resistance and accommodation ... A comprehensive understanding of these processes requires a systematic analysis directed to how social-cultural reproduction occurs, shifts its forms, and is remodelled — not merely in whose interest these processes operate. We thus need a youth research which encompasses *the full range* of social individuals, social positions, life contexts, strategies and consequences. Equally necessary, however, is a youth research able to extrapolate structuring principles which can provide sociological explanations for individual biographies. (1990, p.38)

A concept of culture which embraces both the micro and the macro levels of analysis can be found in the field of cultural studies, especially studies of youth cultures (e.g. Hall and Jefferson, 1976; Willis, 1983) influenced by Gramsci's understanding of common sense as the 'concretely lived culture of a particular class or group, influenced both by external ideologies and internally generated understandings' (Gramsci, quoted in Williams, 1985, p.337). For Gramsci, common sense is not uniform: it is 'an ambiguous, contradictory and multiform concept' (Forgacs, 1988, p.346) containing elements of both cultural reproduction and contestation. (See Hall, 1986).

These ideas have informed several recent ethnographic studies of multiracial youth cultures that have illuminated the ways that themes of racism and antiracism may coexist within the same subcultural configuration, and consequently may coexist, contradictorily, in White discourse and consciousness. Of these, the studies by Roger Hewitt (1986), Simon Jones (1988) and Les Back (1991) are of particular importance. Shared experiences and cultural orientations, and cross-racial friendships, do not automatically lead to antiracism. Jones speaks of:

the deeply contradictory nature of White responses about race. In struggling to resolve the contradictions that resulted from their friendships and cultural-musical influences, young Whites constantly had to battle not only against the weight of peer-group pressure, but also against other, more general, ideological influences. (1988, p.219)

I have briefly outlined a framework for looking at 'race' and children's cultures. I now want to turn to my own research.

Conflict in children's cultures

My research was conducted in Years 5 and 6 of three mainly White primary schools. It was largely based on individual and group interviews with 170 children, a total of 246 interviews altogether. Our discussions revealed the key elements of their social world, which can be summarised briefly as follows:

- Friendship: the friendship group and best-friend pair relationships, including conflict among friends — breaking friends and taking friends; competition and exclusion.

- Relations between same-sex peer groups, including hierarchical relations.

- Relations between the sexes: conflict and friendship, including 'romance relations'.

- Relations between older and younger children: conflict and hierarchy, but also caring and protection.

All of these social relationships were structured by the dynamics of equity and dominance. And all of them could become racialised, in two principal ways. The first took the form of aggressive conflict. This consisted predominantly of name-calling and other verbal taunts. I found no evidence of physical racial conflict. The second form of racialisation was patterns of inclusion and exclusion. This took various forms: exclusion from friendship groups; exclusion from activities; racialised gossip which functioned to construct boundaries between social identities; the racialisation of romance relationships. Lack of space prevents me from commenting on all of these here, so I will focus on name-calling and other verbal taunts as the most common and tangible form of conflict, which was also by far the most prevalent form that racism took in the three schools.

Name-calling was a common interaction strategy, often chosen to inflict the maximum hurt. There was widespread agreement among the White children that name-calling about one's family was the most hurtful kind. The most offensive remarks were made either about families splitting up or family members' illness or death. Children in those situations were vulnerable to particularly offensive remarks. Kerry described one such incident.

One of the children was picking on Hayley. Hayley's mum was in hospital, she nearly died, and one of the children was picking on her and saying 'Oh your mum nearly died', and it really upset Hayley.

It is possible to distinguish between two types of name-calling situations. The first is described by Gillian.

G: Well sometimes I've no control over things that I think of.

RH: When does this happen?

G: When they start picking on me and accusing me of something. It just comes out.

'Hot' name-calling like this occurred during heated disputes, often between friends, and afterwards often led to feelings of regret and guilt, and to apologies, though many children felt that the heated emotional state excused or justified name-calling that would otherwise have been regarded as unacceptable calculated harassment. It can be contrasted with 'cold' name-calling situations, in which children deliberately teased or harassed other children for pleasure. For many children, aggressive behaviour, verbal or physical, is fun, as John and Robert explain.

R: I don't live with my mum and dad and I get picked on sometimes because of that.

RH: What do they say?

J: What amazed me was the boy that was picking on him for that, he doesn't have a dad. I couldn't work that out.

RH: Why would they want to say things about not living with your mum and dad?

R: I don't really know, they just like to hurt people really.

J: They like to have an emotional victory on somebody. They think they're the best at everything.

Racist name-calling

I now want to examine situations in which name-calling took a racialised form. Developing the distinction I have made between 'hot' and 'cold' name-calling, I suggest that there are three categories of racist name-calling, and that the difference between them derives from children's different applications of the concept of equality in racialised contexts.

Illegitimate defence

Nicola and Stuart, two White children, spoke to me about calling Asian children racist names.

N: They're alright. You probably talk about them and call them names, which they don't like, but then you like apologise to them or something.

S: Because you say it accidentally and hurt their feelings ...

N: You don't mean to say it. You say something like 'Go and have a wash' or something. It's horrible, you wouldn't like it but it's just like gets on your nerves ...

S: When you get angry it just slips out. You hurt their feelings and you have to go and apologise. It's happened to me ...

RH: Did you apologise?

S: Yes I did.

RH: Why did you?

S: Because it's not very nice — it's not their fault that they are a different colour to us. It's just the way they were born. Older people call them horrible names. We've heard them on the telly and things like that, and we've got them in our minds and then when you get angry with them we say it but we don't mean to.

103

Many children spoke in similar terms of incidents when they had used racist names in what they regarded as self-defence. They explained that racist name-calling occurred as the result of feeling angry or upset, when it just 'came out'. Afterwards they felt sorry that they had said it, because it hurt Black children's feelings unfairly. It is the racial form of 'hot' name-calling that was described earlier. To attack Black children on racial grounds was a breach of the principle of equality because, as Stuart said, 'it's not their fault that they are a different colour to us'. This type of racist name-calling often occurred between children who were friends. Most of the children's peer interaction took place with friends, and friendship relations frequently involved conflict.

Legitimate defence

Not all children regretted using racist name-calling defensively in 'hot' situations. Some saw it as a legitimate tactic in arguments with Black children. This is Katy.

K: I've called racist things ... I called Jagdeep, did I tell you, 'Bobble 07' because they wear bobbles on their heads for their religion, because he was picking on me and then I picked on him and I just called him a name.

RH: Why do you think you called him that particular name rather than just calling him another name not to do with his colour?

K: Because I'd heard people calling him that name and I know he gets upset about it, so if I know he gets upset about it, I call him that name.

She continued by mentioning a time when she had called Claire, an African-Caribbean girl in her class, 'Blacky'.

RH: Is it different calling Claire, say, 'Blacky', from calling her 'cow' or something like that?

K: It's not different, it's just a name. If there's a name about someone then you call it them. If you think they are, then you call it them.

Some children, like Katy, used racist remarks only in what they defined as self-defence in 'hot' situations, but saw it as a legitimate strategy in that context. They had a repertoire of strategies which they applied differentially depending on context. The key criterion for the children was the notion of equality. In situations where the self was under threat, the maintenance of self was regarded as equating to the restoration of equality. The use of racist remarks in those situations, therefore, was legitimate because its purpose was not the creation, but the remedying, of inequality.

Legitimate dominance

One of the most common explanations that children gave for racist name-calling was that it was motivated by the desire to 'act tough'. 'Acting tough' was a term mainly ascribed to boys, though it also applied to girls, perhaps in the form of 'showing off'. Both terms imply that it was seen as a breach of the equality principle. It occurred principally outside the friendship group. The subculture of the friendship group comprised values and strategies for preventing and managing conflict and maintaining relatively egalitarian relationships within the group. Among boys, it was part of the interactional repertoire for establishing a particular type of male identity through the assertion of dominance. This is Nasar's explanation of why some boys used racist name-calling.

> Because they think they'll look good. They think they're the leaders and they can beat everyone.

A boy called Robert exemplified the 'acting tough' model and the use of what he regarded as legitimate racist name-calling as a strategy of self-assertion over others. Robert was notorious for his aggressive behaviour and had been in trouble on several occasions for racist name-calling.

> Oh yes, I call them 'niggers' or 'pakis' or 'chocolate biscuit' or something like that. They've got a lot to put up with. If you've fallen out or something and you see something brown or Black you go 'Oh look there's your cousin over there', like that.

One common context for this form of name-calling was between older and younger children, in the struggle to maintain, and to challenge, the age hierarchy.

Behaviour and belief

I turn now to the question of the relationship between racist behaviour and beliefs about 'race'. Is racist name-calling always expressive of racist beliefs?

Simon was typical of many of the children at the three schools in regarding most racist name-calling, like other forms of name-calling, as purely instrumental, without any necessary underlying racist beliefs. Racist names were no different from other abusive terms. He was asked if children who used racist name-calling really didn't like Black people being in this country.

S: But when I say this, they haven't got such serious feelings about it, they just say it and mocking them and everything. They're not really serious or anything, but they really say it when they get mad or something, or whenever they see them that's what they use against them. The same with Tony, they use against him 'four eyes' and they use against Zabeel 'Paki' and if they use against David they use 'titch' or something. Things like that.

RH: So are you saying that calling somebody 'Paki' or 'go back to your own country' is just the same as saying 'four eyes' or 'titch'?

S: Virtually, yes.

I asked Simon if he would use racist name-calling against, for example, Kevin, a Black boy, if he had an argument with him.

Probably if I had an argument. It's something to use against him isn't it?

Not only White children but all the Black children shared this view. This is Yvette and Natasha.

RH: Do you think, I mean it's difficult to say, do you think they really want you to go away or do you think they are just saying that for something to hurt you?

N: They just want to hurt us.

Y: To get at us.

106

The distinction that children made between the instrumental and expressive functions of racist name-calling is a real one. It is not simply a rhetorical disclaimer of racist beliefs on the part of White children (van Dijk 1987). The existence of racist beliefs cannot be simply read off from incidents of racist name-calling, any more than racist beliefs automatically generate racist name-calling. Society makes available to children a powerfully charged vocabulary of racist terms, but their use, while trading on the negative meanings that they bear, does not necessarily imply a commitment to the racist ideologies from which they derive. Each incident of choosing to use racist name-calling, or choosing not to use it, needs to be concretely analysed to determine the specific combination of the two dimensions of 'belief' and 'behaviour' which it represents.

I found instances of six types of such combinations or 'racial codes'. Each code represented a specific combination of ideological and interactional orientations. The first two codes do not generate racist behaviour, but for very different reasons.

1. - BELIEF - INTERACTION
children who do not hold racist beliefs and who do not use racist taunts.

2. + BELIEF - INTERACTION
children who hold racist beliefs but do not express them in interaction, because of fear of retaliation by Black children or objection by teachers.

The remaining four codes all generate racist behaviour, but with a range of different meanings for the user. In the next case, the racist behaviour is expressive of racist beliefs.

3. + BELIEF + INTERACTION
children who hold racist beliefs and who regard the use of racist taunts as legitimate.

In the last three codes, the motivation is primarily interactional rather than expressive of racist beliefs. However, the interactional meaning of the behaviour is different in each case.

4. - BELIEF + INTERACTION
children who do not hold racist beliefs but who regard the use of racist taunts as legitimate in situations of 'self-defence' only.

5. - BELIEF + INTERACTION
children who do not hold racist beliefs, who regard the use of racist taunts as illegitimate, but who use them in 'hot' situations and regret doing so.

6. - BELIEF + INTERACTION
children who do not hold racist beliefs but who regard the use of racist taunts as legitimate in situations of assertion of dominance.

'Race' in the cultures of White children

Up to now I have focused on specific incidents of racist name-calling taken in isolation. But of course, as emphasised earlier, racism is embedded in a dense web of social and cognitive processes, taking place over time, which comprise children's cultures. Each specific incident is the product of the biographies of the children involved, the history of their relationship, the contexts of other relationships, their 'interactional ideologies', and how they understand and make use of notions of 'race'. A case study of a White girl called Jacky, aged 10, illustrates this complexity.

Jacky was a member of a large friendship group of girls. She told me about an incident that had occurred some while before, between her and Nina, an Asian girl who was a member of the same friendship group.

> I think I said 'Why don't you go back to where you come from' and just called her a 'Paki' and she called me an 'ice cream' and a 'blob'.

Later in the discussion it emerged that Jacky had also said to her 'go back to your own country'. I asked her why she had chosen to call Nina 'Paki'. It is relevant that Jacky was quite a large girl.

> She called me 'ice cream' which means fatty, then I just thought well she's not fat so what can I call her, well she's Black so I'll call her 'Blacky'.

Afterwards they made friends again. Nina's interpretation of the incident, looking back on it (in a separate discussion), was that it probably did not reflect racist beliefs on Jacky's part.

RH: Why did Jacky call you a name? Is it because Jacky doesn't really like Asian people, or...

N: She is nice to me like. She does take me swimming and stuff. She's not bad but she just called me the name, probably because I were having an argument and I were just calling each other names and she called me that.

RH: You mean that she probably doesn't really think that?

N: She probably didn't mean it.

In other words, it could be seen as a typical instrumental 'legitimate defensive' use of racist name-calling. But I want to explore what lay behind it. First, I want to place the incident in the context of Jacky's relationship with Nina. Jacky said that she and Nina often had arguments.

Well me and Nina aren't close. I always argue. I always have loads of fights. We're still friends but we're not close friends like all the others are.

Jacky explained this in terms of incompatible characteristics, of which 'race' was one.

J: We've just got nothing in common at all.

RH: How do you mean you've got nothing in common, like what?

J: Like I'm fat, she's thin. I'm White, she's Black. She doesn't do anything that I do. She doesn't listen to music. She likes Bros group and I hate it. She plays football and I don't. She just doesn't do anything that I do. I talk about boys and all she can do is talk about football.

RH: I don't see how her being Black and you being White — what difference does that make?

J: Well she just doesn't like the same things as I do. She likes to play more with people of her own colour I suppose. It's not being nasty or anything but she just likes to play with people more. She plays with Gurjit a bit and she just plays football with the boys — her own colour. She plays with White people but not as much as she plays with Black people. I think she feels that she can trust them more than White people.

RH: Why do you think she feels that?

J: Well because if like I said, if I have an argument I can call each other names but if she has an argument they can't call her Black because they are Black as well.

Jacky develops a complex argument here. They do not get on because they have nothing in common. Among the things that separate them is ethnicity. It is Nina who makes ethnicity an issue by preferring to play with children of 'her own colour'. But there is a good reason for this: she can trust Black people more because they do not call her racist names. 'Race' helps to provide Jacky with an explanation for why they do not get on.

However, neither the accounts of other children nor research observations support Jacky's view that Nina prefers playing with Black, or Asian, children. On the contrary, Nina was one of the most popular girls in the large group of girls, the rest of whom were White, and her best friend for over a year, with whom she was very close, was a White girl. She did regularly play football at playtime, but most of the children who played, mainly boys, were White. Jacky has constructed a racialised and distorting interpretive framework which recursively both serves to explain her problematic personal relationship with Nina and appears to receive confirmatory sanction from it.

To explain the motivation that sustained that racialised interpretive lens we need to place the relationship between Jacky and Nina in the context of the relationships among the girls in the group. There was competition for friendships within the group, and Jacky felt particularly vulnerable to exclusion, as Nina explains.

RH: Is Jacky a friend of yours?

N: Yes, she's one of my best friends but I don't get on well with her. Well none of us get on well with her.

RH: Why is that?

N: Because if I start walking together and talking to each other and telling each other secrets she starts crying. I don't know why but I say 'We'll tell you after' and she just goes 'Well I'm not your friend' and she starts crying.

RH: Is that because you're leaving her out of things?

N: Well I weren't leaving her out, I were just talking to each other and she thought that I were leaving her out.

RH: Does this happen quite a lot?

N: Yes.

RH: Is that because she'd like to be really best friends do you think, more than she is at the moment?

N: I think she wants to be more than any of us.

Jacky herself revealed her insecurity over friendship relations in the group when talking to me about her relationship with Hannah, her best friend.

J: When she is with other people I think she tends to be really hard. When she's on her own she's really nice. And that is when I mostly fall out, when she is with somebody else and I am in a group of three or four, because she starts just laughing like all the life is shut up inside, and then when other people go away she just opens the gate and she's nice again.

RH: When you say she is hard, what do you mean?

J: It's like when she is with people, not her mum or dad or her brother, when she is with her other friends, just like she changes. Like she gets a hard coating on the outside like gates, and then when she is with me she just opens the gates and cuts the hard coating and she's nice when she is with one person ... When I'm with Hannah I feel more relaxed but when I'm with a group of people I feel that I have to do things right or they will laugh at me. When I'm with one person I know that I can trust Hannah, I just feel alright.

The insecurity that informs Jacky's relationships with her White friends also extends to, and assumes a racialised form in, her relationships with Black children.

J: I like some of them. It's just that some of them I don't feel right when I'm with them.

RH: Really, how do you mean?

J: I feel on edge all the time and that I can't talk to them.

When I asked her why this was so, she qualified her remarks.

J: Well Jasmine, she's Asian I think, I can talk to her a little like but she's fun to be with. Some of them are fun to be with but it's the ones that are really mardy [moody] or don't like doing things that I don't get on with. I get on with most of them.

At this point the connection between her understanding of her personal relationships and her more general views about 'race' began to become clear. When I asked her whether her remark to Nina, 'Go back to your own country', represented her real views about Black people she said 'Black people who weren't born here should go back to their country they were born in'. I asked her why she felt that.

J: Well it's just the ones I don't get on with. I think that if they don't get on with everybody, that if they were born somewhere else, if they wanted to come over here that they have got to try and and get on and not be nasty to people they've just come to meet.

RH: White people you mean?

J: Yes. And some of them, the ones I don't like, they're just nasty and think that they own the country. Like the White people think that no-one owns it and they let the people come in and then they just cheat them and they can come in whenever they want.

RH: Who are you thinking of when you say this? Are you thinking of children at this school or people outside?

J: People outside mainly, because you're walking down the street and you see a Black person and they just start, if they're older and thin and they're perfect, and they see somebody fat coming down the street they call them 'Fatty'.

RH: Does that happen to you?

J: Yes.

RH: And what did you think?

J: I thought like saying 'Why don't you go back to where you come from?'

RH: Was this a boy or a girl or a man or a woman who said it?

J: Well it's usually teenagers. It's usually boys and girls.

RH: Is it usually Asian or West Indian or both?

J: Both. No, I don't think Black people call it so much, but the brown they call it me quite a lot.

This case study of Jacky is a revealing example of how common-sense racist ideas achieve their purchase within the cultures of children by their ability, as Hall and Miles suggested, to provide apparently convincing explanations of, and ways of coping with, real-life problems. In the case of Jacky this can be seen working at the most personal level, embedded in and motivated by the unhappiness that peer relations can cause her. Racialised explanations of her own interpersonal relationships and experiences, and common-sense racist ideas about 'race' and nationality drawn from the wider society, feed into and mutually confirm each other. There are racist elements in Jacky's thinking, certainly, but they coexist and conflict with a more egalitarian dynamic. She is concerned to affirm her own equality; but her qualification of her judgements about Black people and her recognition of racial discrimination also reflect her attempts to apply the principle of equality in the treatment of people to her experiences.

Further research is needed in order to build up a more comprehensive set of case studies of racism among children which would be capable of supporting more extensive empirical generalisations and of providing the basis for a more developed theorisation than I have attempted here. With regard to racist name-calling, I have suggested six 'racial codes' which may serve at least as an initial explanatory model for subsequent research. In terms of more extended case studies, such as that of Jacky, more research is needed before we can identify more confidently what is generalisable and what is idiosyncratic, and generate a productive set of middle-range analytic concepts. What I would claim, however, is that this study provides convincing confirmation of the validity of the two theoretical perspectives, one concerning 'race', the other concerning the cultures of children, which I outlined and brought together at the beginning of this chapter.

Finally, the findings of this research have important implications for teachers and others concerned to tackle racism among children. I would briefly make three points:

- 'Race' is a significant feature of children's lives, White as well as Black, and needs to be specifically addressed.

- 'Race' is embedded in children's cultures, and therefore it needs to be tackled as part of a much broader project by schools, to help children to understand their own lives, relationships, experiences, ideas and social behaviour. Many children demonstrate considerable insight into these issues, which teachers can build on.

- The existence of contradictory elements in Jacky's thinking and in her experience, coupled with the insight she shows, was typical of many of the children I interviewed. Sensitively helping children to uncover and work through those inconsistencies and contradictions is a vital part of antiracist teaching.

Acknowledgement

This chapter is based on research carried out by Richard Hatcher and Barry Troyna and funded by the ESRC (Reference X204252006).

Chapter 7

Using habitus to look at 'race' and class in primary school classrooms

Diane Reay

Introduction

There have been very few attempts to utilise Bourdieu's concept of habitus in empirical work (Atkinson, 1983, Delamont, 1989; McClelland, 1990; Engler, 1990). However, my own research employs habitus as a method for exploring the dominance of dominant groups and the domination of subordinate groups within the context of primary school classrooms. From February 1993 until June 1994 I spent at least one day a week as a participant observer in two urban primary schools. Oak Park, in an outer London borough has a social composition which is largely White and middle class. Milner, three miles to the south, is predominantly working class, with a multi-ethnic intake. The names of the two schools and those of children and parents discussed in this article are pseudonyms.

My research interest lay in operationalising Bourdieu's concept of habitus as a method for analysing peer group interaction. I specifically wanted to look at how power is manifested among pupils in the classroom. Elsewhere I investigate the mutual influences of gender, 'race' and class on pupil peer group cultures (Reay, 1991; 1995). However, in this chapter my primary focus is on intersections of 'race' and social class, although gender inevitably permeates my descriptions of the two classrooms. In particular, I examine the practices generated by White, middle class habitus as they seem to be held up for scrutiny far less than those of less advantaged groups in society. Aaron Cicourel suggests that one potentially rewarding application of habitus is as a tool for examining domination as everyday practice (Cicourel, 1993a, p.111) and I have attempted to do this in my own analysis. Before discussing my empirical work, I describe how habitus can be utilised as a method and outline my understanding of racialised habitus. First, I sketch out the elements of habitus as theory, drawing out four key features of the concept: its emphasis on embodiment, the complex interplay between past and present, the tension between collective and individual trajectories, and its integration of agency with structure.

Habitus as theory

Pierre Bourdieu's concept of habitus has been widely critiqued (Jenkins, 1992; Brubaker, 1993; Robbins, 1991; Sewell, 1992; Harker et al 1990; Cicourel, 1993a; 1993b). Most of the critiques have focused on the ambiguity of the concept. Roger Brubaker states that Bourdieu's concept of habitus is not intended to be 'precise or unambiguous' (Brubaker, 1993, p.217), while Bourdieu, in an interview with Loic Wacquant, states: 'I do not like definitions much' (Bourdieu and Wacquant, 1992, p.95). This results in problems of indeterminacy and changing notions of habitus in Bourdieu's writing. Paradoxically, the conceptual looseness of habitus also constitutes a potential strength. It makes possible adaptation rather than the more constricting straightforward adoption of the concept within empirical work. There is also a 'messiness' about the concept that fits in well with the complex messiness of the real world. I would suggest that it is the aspects of habitus that remain relatively unfilled, what Jenkins has described as 'the processual and ontological mysteries of the habitus (Jenkins, 1992, p.130), that simultaneously contain its seductions and its pitfalls.

Bourdieu has developed the concept of habitus to demonstrate not only the ways in which the body is in the social world but also the ways in which the social world is in the body (Bourdieu, 1981):

> The habitus as the feel for the game is the social game embodied and turned into a second nature. (Bourdieu, 1990b, p.63)

Thus, one of the crucial features of habitus is that it is embodied; it is not composed solely of mental attitudes and perceptions. Bourdieu writes that it is expressed through durable ways 'of standing, speaking, walking, and thereby of feeling and thinking' (Bourdieu, 1990a, p.70). For Bourdieu, key aspects of culture are embodied. This is a repeated theme in his work. He describes the dispositions that make up habitus as 'meaning-made-body' (Bourdieu, 1990a, p.43). In his empirical study of French society there are many references to the ways in which difference in habitus results in different ways of talking, eating, walking and exercising. Indeed the way in which individuals treat their bodies 'reveals the deepest dispositions of the habitus' (Bourdieu, 1984, p.190).

Bourdieu describes his development of the concept of habitus as an attempt to overcome the latent determinism in structuralist theory (Bourdieu, 1985a). He views the concept as central to his aim of developing a theory of action. However, the addendum in Bourdieu's work is always an emphasis on the constraints and demands which impose themselves on people. While the habitus allows for individual agency, it also predisposes individuals towards certain ways of behaving:

> The habitus, as a system of dispositions to a certain practice, is an objective basis for regular modes of behaviour, and thus for the regularity of modes of practice, and if practices can be predicted ... this is because the effect of the habitus is that agents who are equipped with it will behave in a certain way in certain circumstances. (Bourdieu, 1990b, p.77)

Despite this implicit tendency to behave in ways that are expected of 'people like us', for Bourdieu there are no explicit rules or principles which dictate behaviour, rather *'the habitus goes hand in hand with vagueness and indeterminacy'* (Bourdieu's own italics, 1990b, p.77). The practical logic which defines habitus is not one of the predictable regularity of modes of behaviour, but instead that of vagueness, of the more-or-less, which defines one's ordinary relation to the world (Bourdieu, 1990b, p.78).

Bourdieu views the dispositions, which make up habitus, as the products of opportunities and constraints framing the individual's earlier life experiences. They are:

> durably inculcated by the possibilities and impossibilities, freedoms and necessities, opportunities and prohibitions inscribed in the objective conditions. (1990a, p.54)

As a result, the most improbable practices are rejected as unthinkable but, concomitantly, only a particular range of possible practices is considered. Choice is at the heart of habitus, which he likens to 'the art of inventing' (Bourdieu, 1990a, p.55), but at the same time the choices inscribed in the habitus are very clearly limited.

It is difficult to decipher the extent to which the habitus of individuals in the same group converge. A person's individual history is constitutive of habitus but so also is the whole collective history of family and class that the individual is a member of. At times then, Bourdieu seems to be suggesting a degree of uniformity. However, at other times, he recognises differences and diversity between members of the same cultural grouping and writes in terms of the singularity of individual habitus (Bourdieu, 1990a, p.60). Habitus, within, as well as between, social groups differs to the extent that the details of individuals' social trajectories diverge from one another. Bourdieu attempts to justify his collective definition of habitus. In reference to class habitus he asserts that:

> interpersonal relations are never, except in appearance, individual-to-individual relationships and that the truth of the interaction is never entirely contained in the interaction. (1990b, p.81)

A collective understanding of habitus is necessary, according to Bourdieu, in order to recognise that individuals contain within themselves their past and present position in the social structure 'at all times and in all places, in the forms of dispositions which are so many marks of social position' (1990b, p.82).

Individual histories are therefore vital to understanding the concept of habitus. Habitus is permeable and responsive to what is going on around it. Current circumstances are not just there to be acted upon, but are internalised and become yet another layer to add to those from earlier socialisations:

> The habitus acquired in the family is at the basis of the structuring of school experiences: ... the habitus transformed by the action of the school, itself diversified, is in turn at the basis of all subsequent experiences ... and so on, from restructuring to restructuring. (Bourdieu, 1972, cited in Bourdieu and Wacquant, 1992, p.134)

Therefore, although the habitus is a product of early childhood experience, and, in particular socialisation within the family, it is continually modified by individuals' encounters with the outside world (Di Maggio 1979). Schooling, in particular, acts to provide a general disposition, a turn towards what Bourdieu terms 'a cultured habitus' (Bourdieu, 1967). Thus, while habitus reflects the social position in which it was constructed, it also carries within it the genesis of new creative responses which are capable of transcending the social conditions in which it was produced. Habitus is 'the product of social conditionings, and thus of a history' (Bourdieu, 1990, p.116). The range of possibilities inscribed in a habitus can be envisaged as a continuum. At one end habitus can be replicated through encountering a field that reproduces its dispositions. At the other end of the continuum, habitus can be transformed through a process that either raises or lowers an individual's expectations. Implicit in the concept is the possibility of a social trajectory which enables conditions of living that are very different from initial ones.

By drawing together these four themes running through Bourdieu's discussions of habitus, habitus can be viewed as a complex internalised core from which everyday experiences emanate. It is the source of day to day practices. Habitus produces action but, because it confines possibilities to those possible for the social groups the individual belongs to, those actions for tend much of the time to be reproductive rather than transformative. Dispositions are inevitably reflective of the social context in which they were acquired.

Habitus as method

For Bourdieu the chief strength of concepts lies in their empirical relevance (Bourdieu, 1991, p.252). Furthermore, the difficulties and inconsistencies inherent in habitus can be viewed as far less problematic if habitus is viewed as method rather than theory (Hage, 1994). Bourdieu sees his concepts as in a continual process of being reworked:

> The core of my work lies in the method and a way of thinking. To be more precise, my method is a manner of asking questions rather than just ideas. This, I think is a critical point. (Bourdieu, 1985, quoted in Mahar, 1990 p.33)

Habitus is one of the main concepts of his method. He describes the concept as developing out of an interest in understanding how individuals are moulded by social structure (Mahar, 1990). Bourdieu, writing of his conceptual framework, comments:

> I blame most of my readers for having considered as theoretical treatises, meant solely to be read or commented upon, works that, like gymnastics handbooks, were intended for exercise, or even better, for putting into practice; that is, as books that put forth so many programs for work, observation, and experimentation ... one cannot grasp the most profound logic of the social world unless one becomes immersed in the specificity of an empirical reality. (1993a, p.271)

The appeal of habitus for me is that it lends itself to a focus on social inequalities, but one that demands a complex analysis which both recognises diversity within social groupings and highlights the crucial importance of the context in which actions take place. Furthermore, habitus permits an analysis of social inequality which is not solely rooted in location. At the centre of the concept are the social practices, which are the outcomes of an interaction between a habitus and a field. The focus is as much on process as on position. Such an understanding of habitus supports Cicourel's assertion that a productive way of employing habitus in empirical research is as a tool for exploring domination in everyday practice (Cicourel, 1993a, p.111). Cicourel suggests habitus can be used to explore:

> how the child acquires a sense of his or her own power and that of adults and peers, as he or she is assigned and assumes different

relationships within and outside the family, peer and school settings. (1993a, p.109)

As such, habitus provides a way of examining how children use language and physical and emotional displays to dominate or subordinate themselves to others (Cicourel, 1993b).

In his own work, Bourdieu uses habitus as a method for uncovering actors' relationships to dominant culture and the ways in which these relationships are expressed in a range of activities, including eating, speaking and gesturing (Bourdieu, 1984). In a parallel process, I would suggest that habitus can be used as a way of exploring children's relationships to dominant culture through non-verbal behaviour and use of language. Bourdieu's most recent work (Bourdieu, 1993b) looks at the resulting 'misery of position' for people whose habitus is discordant with their position in the social field. In my own research, children were primarily in settings normal 'for people like them' (Bourdieu, 1990a, p.56). However, I have also attempted to use habitus as a method for examining disjuncture between individual and social context as in the case study of the Black, working class child in a predominantly White, middle class school.

Habitus provides a method for simultaneously analysing 'the experience of social agents and ... the objective structures which make this experience possible' (Bourdieu, 1988, p.782). Using habitus as method ensures that the research focus is always broader than the social activities of the classroom. While it is important to view children as actively engaged in creating their social worlds, Bourdieu's method emphasises the way in which 'the structure of those worlds is already predefined by broader racial, gender and class relations' (Bourdieu and Wacquant, 1992, p.144).

Racialised habitus

LiPuma points to a gap in Bourdieu's work where there should be an explication of how 'race' shapes habitus:

Where recent social theory has focused on the way in which regional identities, race and ethnicity are critical to the cultural construction of culture, such forms have no place in the theory of culture based on concepts of field, capital and habitus. (1993, p.23)

LiPuma asserts that in order to explain Bourdieu's own social trajectory from a peasant background in rural Bearn to eminent Professor of Sociology:

> Bourdieu needs an account of why the internalisation of objective possibilities is socially relative, of how the internalisation processes are organised along gender, ethnic, racial and regional lines. (1993, p.24)

I mentioned earlier that embodiment is a key component of habitus. It also shapes its relevance to issues of 'race' and gender. Bourdieu describes king, banker and priest as hereditary monarch, financial capitalism or the Church made flesh (Bourdieu, 1990b). In so doing, I suggest he sets up possibilities for different ways of theorising the situation of women and of people, male and female, from different ethnic groupings. Female habitus can be surmised as a complex interlacing of the dispositions, which are the consequences of gender oppression, with those that are the product of varying levels of social privilege. Similarly, a recognition of racial oppression would inform understandings of racialised habitus. Prejudices and racial stereotypes ingrained in the habitus of members of dominant groups can affect the life chances of any group which is clearly different in some way. The collective social history of different groups in society informs their understandings of the social world and the dispositions and predispositions embedded in collective habitus. Habitus as embodied history would appear to be important in understanding racialised habitus. As Bourdieu points out:

> The reaction of an individual to another is pregnant with the whole history of these people and their relationship. (Bourdieu and Waquant, 1992, p.124).

As I highlighted in the introduction, habitus is primarily a method for analysing the dominance of dominant groups in society and the domination of subordinate groups. As such, Katherine McClelland asserts that:

> it can easily be applied to the analysis of gender (or racial and ethnic) disadvantage as well. (1990, p.105)

Habitus can be used to focus on the ways in which the socially advantaged and disadvantaged play out attitudes of cultural superiority and inferiority ingrained in their habitus in daily interactions. As McClelland asserts, such dispositions are influenced by 'race' and gender as well as social class. I would suggest that taking whiteness for granted is integral to self-evident understandings of the social world embedded in the habitus of White people.

While Bourdieu has begun to write about gendered habitus (Bourdieu, 1990c), he makes no mention of the way in which habitus is differentiated by 'race'. However, it is possible from his extensive writing on the concept to develop an understanding of habitus as shaped by 'race'. In 'The Social Space and the Genesis of Groups', Bourdieu touches on the importance of 'race' to understandings of habitus:

> The social world ... may be practically perceived, uttered, constructed, according to different principles of vision and division — for example, ethnic divisions. (Bourdieu, 1985b, p.726)

Bourdieu goes on to assert that class differences mediate ethnicity resulting in ethnic groups being hierarchically arranged in social space. However, by turning his argument around, it could equally be argued that 'race' differences mediate social class, with the result that Black and White individuals belonging to the same class grouping are allocated differentially in social space according to their 'race'.

Bourdieu describes habitus as 'a system of dispositions common to all products of the same conditionings' (1990a, p.59). As such it can just as readily be understood in terms of 'race' and gender as social class. My investigation of social processes in the primary classroom is an attempt both to explore the power dynamics operating within the peer group and to begin to expand understandings of Bourdieu's concept of habitus to include the influences of 'race' and gender alongside those of social class.

Acting Powerfully: Habitus in the classroom

There were striking differences in the way in which the peer group hierarchies operated in the two schools in which I undertook participant observation. While in working class Milner there were regular displays of power, based on gender and 'race', they were frequently contested and challenged. Sometimes Lucy and Cerise, one a Black working class girl, the other a White working class girl, assumed a stance of 'superiority' in relation to the 'silliness' of the boys in the classroom. A number of times they confided that they found the boys irritating. Cerise commented: 'The boys act younger than their age', and once, when some boys were throwing unifix, Lucy told me 'not to take any notice they are just being stupid." However, at other times they formed a threesome with Stuart, a mixed race boy, collaborating over work and even telling me 'what a nice boy he was'. Girls like Cerise and Lucy often spent time helping less able girls and boys with their work.

Perhaps unsurprisingly, considering that most of the bright boys from more affluent backgrounds had left at the end of year three for the private sector, there was a greater social dichotomy between boys and girls in Oak Park. Melinda told me "I'd die if I had to sit with a boy', while Negar pleaded with Mrs Symmonds 'Whatever you do, don't put me next to a boy'. Throughout the course of my field work, the girls only ever sat next to one boy, Oliver, who on the NFER test scores was by far the cleverest boy in the class.

There were occasions when I noted open displays of racism in Milner. On a class outing, Mandy, the classteacher, told Carly, a White girl, to hold the hand of Daisy, a refugee from Senegal newly arrived in the class. The moment Mandy turned her back, Carly withdrew her hand and wiped it on her skirt, to the disapprobation of Rosetta, who is Black. With a despising glare at Carly, she took Daisy's hand herself. Cerise and Lucy, who had also noticed, exchanged glances of disapproval. 'Race' was part of the overt curriculum in Milner. I have three sets of field notes outlining complaints to the classteacher that a child (in all three cases, boys) was being racist. Alliances were frequently formed on the basis of sex, less often along lines of 'race'. However, what characterised peer group hierarchies in Milner was flux. Hierarchies shifted across space, for example, from the classroom to the playground, and over time.

The gang of four

In Oak Park, the peer group hierarchy was much more constant over time and space. This was largely due to the status of the 'gang of four', a group of White, middle class girls, and their reputation, rooted partly in reality, partly in mythology, among both the children in 5S and their parents. Below are some of the comments made by parents about the gang:

Francis: I think Melinda's doing well. I think the peer group has helped.

Geoffrey: There's a group of bright girls, the gang of five, I think they're called. They work well together.

Maureen: Susan is very, very keen to go to Margaret MacMillan because there's this gang of clever girls, who are going. But with this lot there's so many girls all trying to be friends and they all want to sit on the same table — that's the problem. There have been lots of arguments about who sits where ever since Susan's been in the juniors. It's terrible there's been so much falling out and arguing about who sits on this one table.

Linsey: When she first started in Year 3 her teacher told me Sophie should be up with those girls, I think they're called 'the gang', the very bright ones, who sit near the front. I mean she could be absorbed into the gang if she tried to push herself academically. I mean this gang that has come up through the school and are very, very clever. The teacher told me she should be up there with them, she should be pushing herself, but she hasn't. She's been quite happy to sit just behind them. She has never been competitive in the sense of wanting to be as good as them.

Manju, the mother of one of three Asian children in the class, gives an historical account of the continued power of this group and their social exclusivity:

Last year there was a problem because Negar was inadvertently put on a table where she was ostracised. There's this group of girls, who call themselves the gang. This is an exclusive group of girls, who probably mix out of school. At the time Negar was sitting at their table feeling very isolated and very alienated, very unhappy about going to school. They ignored her, excluded her from all of their activities. She didn't dare say anything to the teacher and I actually had to go into school and say 'Negar is very unhappy on this table, she is very insecure. She is frightened and intimidated by the other girls,' and the teacher acted on it and moved her. Since then the change in her has been marvellous.

In spite of the gang's exclusivity, or paradoxically because of it, enormous amounts of Susan and Melinda's time and energy were directed at becoming a member of the gang. Susan, the only White working class girl in the class, battled relentlessly to be incorporated into 'the gang'. She confided in me 'they are my best, best friends in the whole wide world. I don't want to sit anywhere else.' Melinda told me 'I'll die if Mrs Symmonds puts me on a table with the boys. I want to sit on the clever girls' table.'

Initially, I was mislead by the fiction perpetrated in both the children's and their mothers' accounts that these girls were the cleverest in the class. However, half way through the field work I was given the entire class's NFER test results in Maths, English and Verbal Reasoning. The irony was that the gang were not the cleverest girls in the class. According to the NFER scores, five other girls had better results, than the highest scoring member of the gang. On the test results Susan and Melinda were doing better than two of the gang, while Negar was doing better academically than all four.

The status of the gang was grounded not in academic excellence but rather in social distinction. The girls' confidence, poise, and the affluence of their family backgrounds counted as much as academic achievement. If social desirability was coterminous with academic excellence, then the most popular child in the class, along with Sophie, should have been Josie. However, Josie was a 'loner' within the confines of the peer group, only relating to two or three of the other girls, and seen by the majority of the girls in the class as awkward and socially inept. Instead, social power resided in the gang and a lot of female peer group bartering was directed towards inclusion within this group.

Parents were drawn into this power play. Both Linsey, Sophie's mother and Charles, Robyn's father, came into school to petition for their child to sit with 'the gang'. There are no examples of Milner mothers going into school to negotiate who their child sat with in the classroom. Linsey told Mrs Symmonds 'Sophie is very unhappy about being moved away from her friends.' Robyn led her father into the classroom early one morning so he could state her case for sitting with the gang. I am suggesting that what is at issue here is social distinction. It was the sense of being denied the social status they desired that caused in Susan, Sophie and Melinda's unhappiness.

Neither Sophie's nor Susan's bid for the power bestowed through membership of the gang, was successful. Susan's marginalisation, the way in which the gang 'put her in her place', was graphically highlighted through a play the gang mounted on their own initiative. Initially rejected as a member of the cast, Susan pleaded repeatedly for inclusion. In the end she was rewarded with a non-speaking, non-human part. Her mother, Maureen painstakingly made her costume. On the day of the performance, the gang, augmented by Sophie and Melinda in minor parts, acted out their roles, while Susan, playing a mouse, scampered round the edge of the stage.

Bourdieu writes that:

> The pursuit of distinction — which may be expressed in ways of speaking or the refusal of misalliances — produces separations intended to be perceived or, more precisely, known and recognised, as legitimate differences, which most often means differences in nature (natural distinction). (1985b, p.730)

An analysis of the gang's treatment of both Negar and Susan shows that these girls' pursuit of distinction was achieved through exclusionist practices in which 'race' and class were unspoken frames of reference for designating social acceptability. I would suggest that in relation to the gang of four, the conditions of entry tacitly and practically required for membership (Bourdieu, 1983, p.324) were to be White, middle class and female.

Temi

The strategies of exclusion operating in 5S became most apparent when Temi joined the class. She suddenly appeared one morning, dressed rather shabbily in a jumper and leggings, which made a stark contrast to the other children's smart uniforms. She looked painfully nervous, eyes darting around the room. The teacher was surprised; no one had informed her that a new child was starting. She was clearly cross about not being fore-warned. After a perfunctory glance, most of the children went back to their Maths work, except for Nancy, who looked genuinely surprised at having another Black child in the classroom. Mrs Symmonds, catching Nancy's eye, asked her if she would mind explaining to Temi what she should be doing, and things seemingly settled back to normal. For the next few weeks I waited and watched, but nothing happened. Apart from Nancy, the other children simply ignored Temi. It was as if she did not exist. There were no racist comments, no overt hostility, there was simply no recognition of Temi's presence at all. Nancy, the only child who seemed to be acting in this context, tried to reconcile two conflictual roles, looking after Temi and being an accepted part of the peer group. In the end her desire for incorporation won out and she too started to ignore Temi, apart from the occasions when Temi was clearly upset or had been bullied in the playground.

In contrast to the children's impassivity, the two adults in the room, the class teacher and myself, tried desperately to compensate. In my field notes, I have recorded conversations with the class teacher, where I optimistically advise that it would make a significant difference if we gave Temi lots of attention. I suggest that adult attention would raise her status with the peer group. It did not. I heard her read at length every day that I went into school. Her reading age went up by leaps and bounds — over two years in the nine months I spent in Oak Park, but her popularity with the peer group remained zero. Frankenberg, in her work on 'race', stresses the importance of conceptualising in terms of the whiteness of White women (Frankenberg, 1993). Similarly, these privileged White children in Oak Park have a habitus which has been, and continues to be, power-fully structured by their 'race' as well as their social class. The habitus of the peer group was one in which these children were already working on their social status. They were actively cultivating social distinction. Nancy and the small number of Asian children in the classroom clearly felt unable to risk their social position by supporting Temi, so they too ignored her.

Thus the peer group habitus operated to keep Temi invisible, through processes so subtle they were barely discernible. For weeks I puzzled over what was, or rather, was not, happening. There were no tangible signs of discrimination. It was when I began to focus specifically on silences and absences in the classroom context that I came to an understanding of the social practices underpinning Temi's exclusion. The racism of these middle class children was not manifested in any action; rather, it lay in the absences. Paradoxically, it was there in what was not there, in the lack of care, lack of contact, lack of recognition. Bell hooks has written about the way in which the absence of recognition is a strategy that facilitates making a group 'the other' (1992, p.167). In describing slavery in the American south she asserts that:

> These looking relations were reinforced as Whites cultivated the practice of denying the subjectivity of Blacks (the better to dehu-

manise and oppress) of regulating them to the realm of the invisible. (1992, p.168)

The cost to Temi of these exclusionist strategies is difficult to estimate. When the teacher asked all the children to write down two children they felt they could work well with and two children they would like to sit next to, unsurprisingly, no one mentioned Temi. She wrote on her slip of paper to the teacher 'I don't want to sit next to anyone because no one wants to sit with me but please can I be next to your table.' I would suggest that ingrained in the habitus of these privileged children were prejudices and racial stereotypes which generated their exclusionist practices.

I do not want to overlook Temi's agency in these social processes. Socially her options were heavily circumscribed by the other children's behaviour. However, she did successfully attempt to forge alliances with adults in the school while, simultaneously, working extremely hard on the academic curriculum. According to Mrs Symmonds, she made more educational progress over the course of the year than any of the other children in the class. She was also the one child in the classroom who regularly volunteered to tidy up and often stayed behind, ostensibly to tidy up, but also to chat to her teacher. Perhaps more than any other child in 5S, her *habitus* was being transformed by circumstances which were very different from those of the previous educational field she had been in. She had transferred to Oak Park from a primary school which had a predominantly working class intake. Although I have focused on the negative aspects of those changes, Temi did manage to carve out a positive educational agenda for herself. The excerpt from her end of year report that I include below gives some inkling of the 'symbolic violence' (Bourdieu, 1992) committed by her White peers:

> Temi is a very conscientious and persistent student and is always ready to help out in the classroom, having a sense of responsibility missing in many of her contemporaries. She has a remarkable strength of character and resilience and has survived what for her has been a very difficult year cheerfully and without complaint. (Oak Park school report July 1994).

Conclusion

As Bourdieu asserts, all racisms resemble one another (Bourdieu, 1993c, p.179). The racism which comes from being White, no less than the racism he claims is a product of class, is ingrained in habitus and generates social practices. Exclusions of class are compounded by exclusions of 'race' and vice versa. While Susan and Negar are tolerated, I suggest at great cost to their sense of self-worth, Temi transgresses social conventions of both 'race' and class and is excluded.

Habitus is one way of looking at how gender, 'race' and class work in everyday interactions. In *Distinction,* Bourdieu describes many examples of social class embodiment and includes breadth of gesture, elevated posture and slow glances as middle class characteristics (Bourdieu, 1984; Szczelklin 1993, p.14). In 5S, the children demonstrated their social status, but not through any obvious social interaction with each other. Rather, processes of social differentiation were acted out through their bodies, in averted eyes, through turning away, by a failure to hear; in sum, a whole range of bodily gestures which signified that Temi was not important enough to notice. Habitus is, above all, about embodiment and in these White children's responses to Temi we have an illustration of Bourdieu's meaning-made-body (Bourdieu, 1990a, p.43). Social distances are inscribed in the body (Bourdieu, 1987, p.5). The vast distance in social space between Temi and other children in 5S was played out through non-verbal displays of aversion and lack of understanding (Bourdieu, 1987, p.5).

Practices of social and cultural exclusion were as evident in this primary classroom as Lamont found them to be among the French and American male elites she studied (Lamont, 1990). All my writing is informed by a realisation that I write from a particular social location and that my account is just one of many versions. However, my under-standings of habitus in the context of the classroom in Oak Park are mirrored in the concerns expressed by teachers about the way children treated the dinner ladies, the majority of whom were Black. A year four teacher told me: 'the meal supervisors have a hard time here. The children are very dismissive of them', while the Headteacher said:

Sometimes they are very rude to the dinner ladies. They think they are superior, but I won't put up with it. There is never any excuse for rudeness.

Mrs Symmonds confirmed what the other two members of staff had said: 'It's true they don't treat the dinner ladies very well'.

I do not want to make simplistic comparisons. Milner classrooms were not havens of helpful children happily and harmoniously cooperating. They were also characterised by hierarchies in which sexism and racism visibly shaped children's lives. Rather, I want to challenge common-sense and pathological understandings which see the working classes as essentially racist, while the middle classes are presented as 'more enlightened'. (For similar challenges see Cohen, 1992; Troyna, 1993a). While racialised habitus in Milner was manifested through overt displays of racism, the racism of middle class habitus in Oak Park operated through processes of dissimulation. In Oak Park, sexism, racism and classism were far more hidden than in Milner. They functioned beneath a veneer of civility and good manners. However, in the attitudes displayed towards Negar and Susan and in the avoidance of interaction with Temi, there is evidence of the tendency to perpetuate in their being the system of difference and distance constitutive of distinction that Bourdieu asserts characterises middle class habitus (Bourdieu, 1993a, p.274). Habitus incorporates 'a sense of one's place' or what Bourdieu terms, the practical mastery of the social structure as a whole (Bourdieu, 1985b, p.728). However, a sense of one's place is simultaneously a sense of the place of others (Bourdieu, 1987, p.5). Power relations are internalised in the habitus as 'categories of perception' of these relationships (Bourdieu, 1985b, p.728). From the evidence of my research, understandings of power relations are informed not only by social class but also by 'race', in the form of an unconscious, taken-for-granted sense of the superiority of whiteness ingrained in habitus.

Bourdieu writes that the dominant class feel themselves to be essentially superior (Bourdieu, 1993c, p.177). In a similar process, the taken-for-granted superiority of whiteness is part of 'natural', self-evident understandings of the social world embedded in the habitus of White people. I would suggest that Bourdieu places too little importance on the potential of 'race' to structure the social field and mediate the differences of social class that he elaborates throughout his writing. In particular,

131

habitus as embodiment points to 'race' being a crucial component of an individual's habitus. As mentioned earlier, Bourdieu does use the term racism in his work, but he uses it with reference to class (Bourdieu, 1993c, p.23). However, social space is divided up by 'race' as well as class.

In the context of Oak Park, I believe there are equally valid grounds for conceptualising in terms of White racialised habitus which generates an almost unconscious process of ordering individuals in social space according to differences of 'race'. This way of seeing the world, which is mediated by other power relations such as those of gender and social class, already appears to be deeply ingrained in the collective habitus that these White children act out in peer group cultures.

Chapter 8

Reconsidering multicultural/antiracist strategies in education: articulations of 'race' and gender in a primary school

Paul Connolly

Introduction

How we have come to theorise and understand racism and the varied nature and forms of the strategies developed to challenge it have increasingly come under question and critical scrutiny over the past decade (Sivanandan, 1985; Gilroy, 1987, 1990; Cohen, 1988, 1992; Rattansi, 1992). In the field of 'race' and education, a number of important studies have emphasised the complex and contingent nature of Black[1] and Asian students' experiences of schooling and have quite successfully highlighted the wider social context within which racism is produced and reproduced (Wright, 1986, 1992; Mac an Ghaill, 1988, 1994; Gillborn, 1990, 1995; Troyna and Hatcher, 1992; Connolly, 1995a, 1995b). Here,

133

as the Burnage Report so dramatically illustrated (Macdonald et al, 1989), racism is not simply a unified and unproblematic set of beliefs and practices but is inherently contradictory and contingent and can only be understood in terms of how it relates to other systems of inequality including class, gender and sexuality. As Gillborn (1995) so forcefully argues, what such work has done is to draw attention to the very real problems and difficulties faced by teachers in trying to develop antiracist policies in schools and to how much of the earlier literature on policy and practice has been strong on rhetoric and critique and essentially weak on highlighting possibilities and potential ways forward (see also Carrington and Short, 1989; Crozier, 1994).

It is upon the practical problems faced by schools in developing multicultural and antiracist policies that this chapter will focus. It draws attention to some of the difficulties experienced by teaching staff committed to developing racially egalitarian policies and practices in one primary school. We can see how certain strategies, developed with the most laudable intentions and out of very real concerns can, without the appropriate material or practical support, have a number of adverse consequences. More specifically, this chapter explores how one particular strategy, aimed at trying to engage older Black boys in the primary school through sport and particularly football, actually had the consequence of creating an atmosphere and ethos in the school where, ironically, certain forms of racist incidents were more likely to occur. The chapter thus draws attention to the inherently complex nature of racism and how it can only be understood in relation to other forms of inequality, in this instance, gender (see also Davis, 1981; hooks, 1982).

After briefly providing some basic background details regarding the school, the chapter discusses a number of racist incidents amongst the boys in the school, observed during the field work and draws some preliminary conclusions about the types of contexts which render the occurrence of such incidents more likely. The importance of masculinity and sport is then examined in this context, so providing the starting point from which a more detailed and specific analysis of the school's approach to football and Black boys can be considered.

Manor Park Estate and Anne Devlin Primary School

The present chapter draws upon data derived from a year-long ethnographic study of Anne Devlin Primary School. I spent three days a week, on average, observing and interviewing the school's three parallel, vertically-grouped, Reception/Year 1 infant classes (ages 5 to 6).[2] Manor Park Estate, the main catchment area for the school, is a council estate in an English inner-city. As it is surrounded by four main dual-carriageways, the estate is relatively self-contained, with the majority of its housing comprising maisonettes and two imposing tower blocks. Unemployment is high on the estate and there is a noticeably higher proportion of single parent families with very young children. Demographically, whilst the immediate surrounding neighbourhoods contain high proportions of Black and Asian people, the estate itself is predominantly White, with only 14 per cent Asian and 8 per cent Black inhabitants. The incidence of racist attacks on the estate (especially against Asians) is high.

Anne Devlin is a relatively large primary school which had 407 children on roll at the start of the 1992/3 academic year. Because of the demographic variations on the estate, the school itself is more ethnically diverse than its catchment area. Roughly half its children are White, a quarter are Asian and a quarter Black. All children on the estate attend one of the three nursery classes in the school for at least a term full-time before moving up to one of the four[3] Reception/Year 1 classes after their fifth birthday. There are two parallel classes for each respective year except for the top two years (Years 5 and 6) where there is only one class for each; this highlight the significantly younger population on the estate.

Contextualising racist incidents in the school

As a number of ethnographic studies of peer-group relationships have shown, racism is not simply an ahistorical and pre-given reality but is heavily context-specific (Hewitt, 1986; Jones, 1988; Back, 1990, 1991, 1993; Troyna and Hatcher, 1992). From drawing together data derived from direct observations of, and secondary accounts relating to, racist incidents at Anne Devlin, I want to propose two main contexts within which racist incidents are more likely to occur in the boys' peer-group. relations. I am not, however, precluding the possibility that there may be other, equally important, contexts. Nor am I suggesting that there is any simple causality between contexts and actions. Individual children are strategic agents, with their own personal biographies, operating within a complex set of relationships which are evolving and ever-changing. A child's actions can not therefore be simply read off from a particular context but must be understood in terms of the child actively making decisions against a background of the articulation of various macro and micro social processes. The two contexts to be discussed below are therefore not exclusive but should rather be regarded simply as two of the most common situations noted at Anne Devlin in which racist incidents occurred amongst boys.

Competitive situations

The first and most immediate context within which racist incidents were more likely to emerge was in competitive situations. This has been a theme more than adequately discussed elsewhere (Troyna and Hatcher, 1992). Put simply, the more competitive or aggressive relations became, the more likely they were to become racialised. This is illustrated in an incident that occurred early in my field work.

Morning playtime had just ended and the infant children were all lining up to go back inside the school, except for Mrs Scott's Reception/Year 1 infant class. On that day they were lining up by the school gate ready to be led to the Sports Hall for a PE lesson. The Sports Hall was situated in the community centre on Manor Park estate and was about a ten minute walk from the school. Mrs Scott asked me to lead the children at the front whilst she walked at the back. As I arrived at the front, the children were still organising themselves into pairs with two couples of boys (aged five and six years old, one pair both Black, the other with one White and one Black) at the front, arguing and jostling with one another about who should go first. Behind them an Asian boy, Prajay, stood on his own with no-one willing to hold his hand. I took Prajay's hand, went to the front and told the other boys to behave. I then led the children off. As I did so, I could hear one of the Black boys behind me complaining to his friends that Prajay was at the front and, in a slightly raised voice, he said, frustratedly: 'that's it — let the *Paki* go first!'. It was said loud enough for me to hear and prompted me to stop and ask the boy what he had just said. He refused to repeat it, merely re-iterating his complaint that he should have been at the front.

This incident illustrates how a broadly competitive situation arising between a group of boys jostling for position became racialised as the boys' frustrations increased. This competitive, essentially masculine, context and the potential it has for those involved to become increasingly frustrated and angry, and for these relations, then, potentially to become racialised, is particularly true for sport. As will be seen later, sport in the school was generally assigned a high level of importance in assemblies, and the children involved gained much prestige. Whilst this was equally true for all sport, it will be seen that it was football that came to predominate at Anne Devlin and to gain the most attention in school assemblies.

This popularity was also evident in the playground, where teachers and dinner supervisors allowed a number of balls out at playtimes; usually one or two per year group. Over time, certain boys had been entrusted with specific balls — being responsible for taking them out and returning them — and consequently came to regard the balls as their own. So a pattern emerged during playtimes, where the same core groups of boys would be playing together in different parts of the playground. Participation for Asian boys was especially precarious. On the one hand, as will be seen, they were, as a group, systematically excluded from playing by their peers. On the other hand, one Asian boy, Prajay, was allowed to play quite frequently by one group of boys. Prajay was in the same class as these boys and it was because of this that he was let into the game. He had developed more personal and individual relationships with the boys, with the result that he was regarded as 'different' from the other Asian children.

Prajay's position and relationship with the other boys was still highly ambiguous, however. If he did something to upset them he was quickly labelled a 'Paki' again and excluded from playing football. I observed this on two occasions. The first was where he made the mistake of picking up the ball and stopping the flow of the game, for which he was called a 'stupid Paki' by one of two boys who grabbed the ball from him and told him to go away. On another occasion he had successfully tackled another boy and won the ball off him, only to have the boy run after him, push him to the ground and mutter 'Paki', before running off with the ball. Again, what these examples illustrate is the way in which competitive situations often engender feelings of disappointment, frustration and, at times, anger, which then provide the potential for relations to become racialised.

Public spaces

Together with competitive situations, the degree to which relations are public provides the second main context for the emergence of racist incidents. 'Public' here refers to relations involving a larger number of children in more open and visible spaces as opposed to two children, for example, having a 'private conversation' in the corner of the playground. In such public contexts there is much more at stake for children who are continually in the process of constructing and maintaining their identities and status. To lose an argument at any time and in any context was considered serious by the children, but to do so in front of others was seen to be far worse. It is not surprising to find, therefore, that of the handful of arguments that I witnessed between children that resorted to racist name-calling, most had taken place in front of others.

The playground provides a specific arena in which many group activities are played out quite publicly. Not surprisingly, because the playground is host, at any one time during infant playtime, to a potential 150 'spectators', much is at stake. As has been discussed more fully elsewhere, the importance of 'kiss-chase' was one specific activity where the stakes were particularly high (Connolly, 1995b). Here, who a child played with, and consequently who they were willing to be associated with as a boyfriend or girlfriend, was regarded by many children as an integral part of their masculine or feminine identities. The gossip and rumours that continuously circulated amongst peers, surrounding who was 'going out with' whom would often become racialised, as children were teased about going out with 'Pakis' (see Connolly, 1995b, forthcoming).

For boys, sport and most frequently football, provided another arena where the stakes were particularly high. Competence at football, and indeed sports generally, was valued highly amongst the boys and provided one of the central aspects of their masculine identities. Games of football, by their very nature, provided a highly public arena where boys could demonstrate their sporting skills and increase their masculine status. This is possibly where the severe reaction by one boy to being tackled by Prajay, as described earlier, can be located. Not only was the boy 'shown up' and his skills questioned, but he was 'shown up' by a 'Paki' (see also Macdonald et al, 1989). More generally however, Asian boys were almost systematically excluded from playing football. As with kiss-chase, to be seen so publicly playing with Asian boys (or, indeed, with any girls) was

138

to risk lowering one's status. The lack of participation on the part of Asian boys cannot be explained simply in terms of their general disinterest in football. Indeed a number of the Asian boys' parents, when interviewed, mentioned that their sons liked to play football at home with their brothers and sisters. Moreover, one Asian boy, Ajay, had complained to me during one informal conversation we had in the classroom, that Stephen, who is Black, never lets him play. Rather, the Asian boys were, on the whole, actively excluded. This is clear in the following interview where Stephen, Paul (Black), Jordan (Black) and Daniel (White) attempt to justify their exclusion of Asian boys in general whilst allowing Prajay to play at the same time.

PC:	So I'm just trying to figure out who plays [football] — so Prajay plays, does he?
Paul:	Yeah.
PC:	He's one of your's/
Daniel:	/Yeah/
PC:	/What about, er, Ajay and Malde? [both in a parallel Reception/Year 1 class]/
Daniel:	Urrr no!
Paul:	Nah!
Daniel:	They're rubbish!
Jordan:	They're always playing crap games!
PC:	Why are they rubbish though, Daniel?
Daniel:	Because they're Paaa-kis!/
Stephen:	/No, no, no! Because they can't run fast!
PC:	They can't run fast?
Stephen:	Yeah, and say we've got the ball and we just, we just burn it and they're, they're, still near their, near our bloody goal and we and we've got the goal.
PC:	Why can't they run fast?
Paul:	Because they're small! [laughs]
Stephen:	No!

PC: Stephen, you tell us why can't they run fast then?

Stephen: Cos, cos they're Pakis and Pakis can't run fast!

PC: But they're the same as everybody else aren't they?

Stephen: No!

PC: Why? Why aren't they the same as everybody else?

Daniel: Don't know!

Stephen: Cos ...

PC: Well they are, aren't they?

Stephen: [shouting, frustratedly] Cos they're slow and everything!

Jordan: An' they want to be on your side cos you're fast ain't it Stephen?

PC: [...] Would you let Ajay and people play if they wanted to?

Daniel: No!

PC: No? Why not?

Stephen: I wouldn't let slow people play!

PC: But you let Prajay play — is he slow?

Paul: No!

Stephen: He's quite fast!

PC: Yeah but he's Indian!

Stephen: Yeah, so, he ain't got a dot on his head!

Jordan: His mum has!

PC: Yeah but Ajay hasn't got a dot on his head!

Stephen: Yes he has!

Daniel: No he hasn't!

Stephen: He's got a Black one, so there!

The sense in which these six year old children were active agents in making sense of and negotiating their experiences is quite evident here. What the discussion illustrates is the way in which the boys did not simply reproduce the racist views of their parents and/or older siblings but actively took up, re-worked and tailored the general racist discourse about Asians to make sense of and justify their own exclusionary practices (see Connolly, forthcoming).

More generally, from the above discussion of various situations within which racist incidents are more likely to emerge, the centrality of sport as a context for racism is clear. It is a context which brings together a number of key elements in the expression and reproduction of masculine identities. Not only is sport, by definition, highly competitive — regularly resulting in frustration, aggression and disappointment — but these emotions are constantly being played out in a highly public arena, where the need to maintain (masculine) identities and status is felt most acutely. It therefore cuts across both the contexts described above and means in the case of football for example, that not only are Asian boys almost totally excluded from playing by their peers but that the one or two who are occasionally allowed to play are more likely to be at the receiving end of racist name-calling and other verbal, and sometimes physical, abuse. It is this that needs to be borne in mind and which provides the context for examining the school's approach to football and the older Black boys.

Football and Black boys

The present popularity of football in the school is due in part to the appointment of a new headteacher, Mr Redmond, in 1988. The previous headteacher had given it little priority and the existence of a year six football team was solely down to the work of the deputy-head, Mr Pearson. On Mr Redmond's arrival, and especially following the appointment soon afterwards of Mr Wallace, an infant teacher, football played an ever-increasing role within the school. It reflected the three teachers' deep interests in the game and their commitment to foster and develop the game outside of school time. Football practices were arranged after school on four days a week for the juniors; led by Mr Wallace on three days a week, and Mr Redmond on the fourth. Mr Redmond also refereed all matches played at Anne Devlin against other school teams and Mr Pearson remained the 'manager' of the first (year six) team. The interest and enthusiasm for football shown by the head, deputy-head and Mr Wallace was certainly evident in their discussions. They could be seen, on a number of occasions throughout the year, to be deeply engaged in picking the school teams, discussing tactics and going over past games. They did so in informal contexts such as the staff room and in more formal situations, as will be seen later, such as school assemblies. Football therefore remained the main focus of their sporting activities and, thus, also the school's; being arranged, as it was, around a number of school leagues and school knock-out tournaments and covering most of the year.

Football was also a heavily male affair. Although one or two older girls would attend football practices, they were, according to Mr Wallace, treated in a 'hostile and patronising' way by the boys. Furthermore, there were no girls in the main school football teams. Similarly, whilst two or three older Asian boys also attended practice sessions and, on occasion, would be selected for the team, they were very rarely seen playing football at dinner-times with the rest of the older footballing 'elite'. This elite comprised mainly the boys who played for the school teams, who would regularly take up most of the playground during play and especially dinner times with their games of football. Such games were highly organised and heavily policed — there were, after all, reputations to keep.

The footballers also provided the focus and role-models for younger, infant boys, whose own interest in football, according to a number of teachers, had significantly increased since the appointment of Mr Redmond. Football amongst infant boys had been transformed from an essentially marginal affair, with one or two footballs out in the playground at any time, to an increasingly central one. Three or four footballs were now out during most infant playtimes and were heavily controlled and sought after by the boys.

What was striking about the main footballing elite, however, was the significant over-representation of Black boys (see also Carrington, 1983; Jones, 1977). Whilst they constituted around a quarter of the school's population, they formed the majority of the footballing elite — around three-quarters of those involved. In many ways, then, when teachers and other school staff referred to the footballers, they were predominantly referring to Black boys. Moreover, as will be seen from some of the interviews with staff, these were the same boys considered to be amongst the most 'difficult' and disruptive in the school — the most likely to exhibit behavioural problems. And it is here that one significant strand of the school's 'multicultural/antiracist' strategy can be located. For, whilst teachers never overtly labelled it as such, football was being used as one specific strategy in a sincere attempt to engage these Black boys and reduce their perceived disaffection with the school. This is apparent in the following transcript taken from an interview with the headteacher, Mr Redmond. We had just been discussing the view put forward by some of the other teachers that boys should not be allowed to play football for the school if they had misbehaved in school.

PC: And why, generally, are you against using it [football] as a sanction?

Mr Redmond: Erm, because we regard it as part of the school. I think we've got other sanctions that are more effective and there's a danger that if you take away all of the positive things, that the children have got nothing to, nothing to want to work in school for. They don't see they're getting anything out of school and when you get to that position you are in trouble because there's no incentive to behave properly in the first place. So you're around to the totally negative system of managing that child's behaviour. So we like to try and keep it apart if we possibly can and we do do that. Er, and again if the child has been misbehaving in that one area it's actually a chance for them to have a normal relationship, and a positive relationship, with a teacher, which can be helpful in actually getting them back onto — feel a bit more positive about themselves — and back on to sort of behaving better as well.

Mr Redmond's commitment to fostering and developing what he called these 'positive relationships' with the mainly Black boys was apparent in other contexts. During dinner times, for instance, he would occasionally come out into the playground and join the footballers, either chatting with them about football or other such matters or, on occasion, actually playing football with them[4]. When I asked Mr Redmond about this he commented:

It's quite nice for me to get out of the staffroom if you like and, you know, have a bit of a kick about. Erm, it's not a sort of, you know, one of the lads sort of thing, but it is a nice, enjoyable time where we can have a chat about football. Er, maybe seeing me in a bit more of a human light.

One of the more significant effects of all of this was to create a certain masculine ethos or culture within the school; evident between the head, deputy-head and other male staff (particularly Mr Wallace) and including some of the older (mainly Black) boys. Primarily, it manifested itself in a form of masculine banter and camaraderie from which female staff, and girls generally within the school, were excluded and which permeated most aspects of school life including, most contentiously, school assemblies. This is illustrated in the following transcript from an interview with Ms Patterson, one of the infant class teachers who was talking about the morning assembly that day. As can be seen, her comments allude to many of the themes at the heart of the resentment, shared by a number of staff, mainly female, about the nature and level of masculine banter that had developed.

Ms Paterson: ... I mean it was just so, there was just so much about football, I mean it just went on for ages and ages and ages and it was all about the Man-of-the Match and the Sportsmanship and how good this sportsmanship was and how wonderful it was and it was like Mr Wallace and Mr Redmond and Mr Pearson having their little joke and it just went on for too long and it was all male-orientated.

The squad stood up — they were all boys. The thing is that these boys who were standing up are the boys that are always in trouble at dinner time and the ones that mess about in the class, but it's totally overlooked. They represent the school even when they can't behave in school, you know, they're the team that stand up in assembly, get certificates, get this, that and the other [...] and I don't see why we should spend, anyway, spend so much time discussing, er, you know in an assembly, an assembly that has got a nursery in there and an infants in there and that those, that it's nothing to do with them — there's no infant football, no nursery football. I mean it's a long, long time. I mean it could be done in a junior assembly if they want to make such a big deal of it. But the thing is, it's because the head takes that assembly and the head's dead into it as well but, you know, I suppose there's no parallel.

PC: Have you had any chance to talk to Stuart [Mr Redmond] about it then?

Ms Paterson: Yeah, I told Stuart what I felt about the terminology and, erm, basically when they were going to play a match, when he was getting the people together in the car he said, 'Come on lads because we want to find erm, we want you to all be good sports*persons,* and laughed at me! Which I mean I suppose it is funny and I'm sure it wasn't meant in any nasty way but if you're going to take that attitude then what's going to change? It's going to carry on being sexist rubbish isn't it? It's going to carry on being all the lads together, get into our cars we're going to drive off and slaughter them, you know. It's just crap! And the thing is it's very competitive: 'we won!' 'we won!' 'we drew!' 'unfortunately we lost' — it's not the fact that you, that they all had a good time.

This level of feeling was shared, to a lesser extent, by a number of other (mostly female) teachers. I asked Mr Redmond about it in another interview and whether he was aware of these sentiments:

Yeah, yeah, yes definitely. But it's sort of, it's a sort of [laughs], erm, I can understand their feelings — especially if they're having problems managing those children themselves — it's the sort of hang them up brigade, you know, sort of [laughs] if you, if you can only nail them to the wall then this child will no longer be a problem. And they're quite right but it's not in the child's interests [laughs] and in actual fact if they can be, if they could probably be more positive with them themselves, and even if they could be positive about their achievements at football, the spin-offs would probably be that they'd actually enjoy those spin-offs — not just the school in general. Erm, you've got, as a head you've got to strike the balance, erm, it's, you get the law and order brigade in teachers just as much as you do in society in general and, you know, I've got to take a broader view sometimes than they have. But I know that, it may be that some people, when they've, when you've got a child that's very difficult, it's a hard job being professional and not taking it personally. And there may be even some resentment that sometimes the child's successful in that way. Erm, they may not realise they're feeling that, but it may be lurking in the background.

Racism, antiracism and masculinity: some concluding remarks

What was evident from observations and interviews with Mr Redmond, Mr Pearson and Mr Wallace was their sincerity and commitment in trying to find a way of engaging the older Black boys and thus reducing their disaffection with the school and fostering a more positive approach to education generally. It also needs to be noted that this was only one, albeit significant, element of their strategy. The fact that they invited me into the school to do my research, and the interest they have expressed in my observations and analysis since, testifies to their commitment, as does the fact that they had invited a number of Black advisors into the school to work specifically with these older children. Their commitment is, therefore, beyond question even if some of their chosen strategies are not.

During my field work, however, I was confronted with a certain irony. Here, on the one hand, is a senior management team trying to engage Black boys through the promotion of football and other sports. This element of their 'multicultural/antiracist' strategy was, in turn, increasing the popularity of football generally amongst the other children, including the infants. Yet when I approached the question of 'where and when are racist incidents more likely to occur?' I was increasingly drawn to focusing on football as a context within which not only were Asian boys almost systematically excluded but also where any Asian boy who was allowed occasionally to play was far more likely to be subject to racist abuse than in other contexts. This was, therefore, the inherent paradox: a 'multicultural/antiracist' strategy targeted at Black boys which, inadvertently, had the adverse effect of increasing the exclusion and racist abuse experienced by Asian boys and fostering a masculine and sexist culture.

It is a paradox that draws attention, quite acutely, to the need for school policies to be more adequately grounded in an understanding of the inherently complex nature of racism and how its expression can only be understood in relation to other systems of inequality, in this case gender. This observation should not, however, be seen as a criticism of the teaching staff at the school. Theirs is a very difficult predicament: they are facing real concerns with little material support or practical guidance on how to deal with them. At a time when funding in education is being cut, particularly in relation to Section 11 staff, and when the demands on teachers' time has significantly increased with the introduction of the National Curriculum and SATs, it is not surprising that teachers will be forced to rely on pragmatic and, at times, 'rough and ready' strategies to deal with the real and pressing concerns that they face with regards to 'race'. As the growing body of literature on 'race' and education has amply demonstrated, racism in British schools is a deeply ingrained and complex social problem. Without the appropriate resources and necessary support, there will be many more teachers like those at Anne Devlin, who have essentially been set up to fail.

Acknowledgements

The above data are drawn from my doctoral research funded by an ESRC Postgraduate Training Award. This chapter is a shortened and revised version of an article that first appeared in *International Studies in Sociology of Education* (Connolly, 1994). I would like to thank the editor of the Journal, Professor Len Barton, and the publishers Triangle Journals Ltd for their kind permission in allowing this version to be reproduced here.

Key to transcriptions

/   interruption in speech

[...] -   extracts edited out of transcript

[text]   descriptive text added by myself to clarify/highlight the nature of the discussion.

...   a pause

Notes

1. 'Black' here refers to those students who have at least one parent of African-Caribbean origin.

2. Children from the three sample classes were interviewed in small groups at least three times each during the year with some being interviewed up to eight times. Children were interviewed in groups, which were chosen on the basis of friendship patterns. They were interviewed in a separate room in the school for between ten and fifty minutes. Interviews were essentially open-ended and non-directive.

3. There were only three Reception/Year 1 classes at the start of the academic year when I conducted my field work and which thus formed the basis of my study. The fourth class was a vertically grouped Year 1/Year 2 class which only reverted back to Reception/Year 1 class in the spring term.

4. He was also observed doing this on the few rare occasions during the summer term when the Year 5 and 6 boys were playing cricket at dinner time. Interestingly, these boys were virtually all the same boys as those who played football.

Chapter 9

How Black children might survive education

Claudette Williams

Introduction

This chapter is concerned with identifying some of the strategies African-Caribbean parents use to prepare young children for a predominantly White Eurocentric school environment. It combines standard survey methods with a methodology rooted in a respect for the tradition of Black 'researcher writers'.

My focus stems from a continued interest in the developments of multicultural, antiracist education and how they intersect with other anti-discriminatory practices, in particular anti-sexist education. The investigation, on which this chapter is based, aimed to explore some of the strategies parents adopt to help their children manoeuvre and survive the experience of school and, drawing on developments in gender education, to see if there are lessons to be learnt from the 'relative' achievements girls have made in some areas of the curriculum. In short, it seeks to answer the question: 'Why it is that some Black children 'survive' school more successfully than others, when 'race' and racism are factors adversely impinging on all Black children?' Could parents, home and the community actively contribute to making Black children's school experiences fundamentally different?

There is a tendency among researchers/writers in this field of enquiry to adopt positions of the 'outsider', depicting Black people, and women in particular, as passive victims of racism. Collins comments:

> As a result, Black women's experiences with work, family, motherhood, political activism, and sexual politics have been routinely distorted in or excluded from traditional academic discourse (Collins, 1991, p.201).

Our exclusion and marginalisation from traditional academic discourse resulted not only in our experiences being distorted and excluded, but also in having only limited opportunities within which to formulate 'our own' theoretical explanations of our lives.

What, however, Black researchers/writers have done is to draw on available cultural forms and representations — songs, music, dance, stories, and myths — which help explain our experiences (the formation of theories!). Researchers/writers, such as Bryant, Dadzie and Scafe (1985), James and Harris (1993), adopt an 'insider's position', and present Black people as actively constructing their histories. This methodology is described by Parmar, as part of a discussion of Black British photographic, literary and visual representation:

> What is evident in the cultural productions of Black women's creativity is the active negotiation between these objective notions of ourselves (as female, Black, lesbian or working class) and the subjective experiences of displacement, alienation and 'otherness'. The marginal ceases to be the *object* of interpretation and illumination: in our own self-referencing narratives we expropriate those bodies of knowledge and theory which are ethnocentrically bound in a relation of dominance to us as post-colonial subjects ... Writing has meant exposing myself, as well as grappling with theories that might enable a different kind of political discourse of identity (1990, p.102).

Bell hooks is another Black feminist researcher who uses this methodology. She describes how she is positioned both in cultural traditions and also in theory/research (1993, p.9):

And yet, like the old ones before me who had been required by circumstance to willingly or unwillingly leave their ancestral home, I left that world of my beginning and entered the strange world of a predominantly White elitist university setting. I took with me to that world, however, ways of knowing and understanding reality I was determined to keep and hold. They were my links to life-affirming Black cultural traditions. And indeed it was the will and ways of the ancestors that sustained me during that time of my life, that sustains me still (1993, p.9).

This study adopts an active insider's position, in which I identify myself as belonging to the group of Black people being studied. Therefore the language used will sometimes be inclusive, and I will draw on collective themes and ideas voiced by Black mothers concerning Black children. Furthermore I maintain that the Black diaspora carries with it values, attitudes, behaviour, songs, beliefs and other memory forms, which Mervin Alleyne (1988) calls 'moral precepts'. These 'moral precepts' provide a bedrock upon which people devise and develop new strategies to sustain themselves in new environments. It is for this reason that I speak of 'researchers/writers'. In particular, the exclusion of African-Caribbean women from traditional sites of knowledge has led women to use literature, everyday behaviour and music as important forms within which to articulate and transport 'moral precepts'. Paula Marshall vividly illustrates the strength and power of the oral tradition within our lives, as a transmitter of 'moral precepts', when she describes the events which occurred in her mother's kitchen:

Once inside the warm safety of its walls the women threw off the drab coats and hats, seated themselves at the large centre table, and drank their cups of tea or cocoa and talked ... they talked — endlessly, passionately, poetically, and with impressive range ... they would indulge in the usual gossip: whose husband was running with whom, whose daughter looked slightly 'in the way' (pregnant) under her bridal gown ... They also tackled the great issues of the time ... the state of the economy ... politics ... wars and rumours of wars ... Then there was home ... The old country ... Poor — poor but sweet. And naturally they discussed their adopted home ... They lashed out at the racism they encountered, they took to task some of the people they worked for ... The talk that filled the kitchen those afternoons was highly functional ... it served as therapy, ... it restored them to a sense of themselves and reaffirmed their self worth (1983, p.12).

Caribbean women's literature provides a rich source, both of 'moral precepts' and of women actively constructing their histories but, in particular, of the expression of women's desires and aspiration for their children (Collins, 1987; Kincaid, 1985; Edgell, 1982; Buffond and Payne, 1990).

Another form of active-insider research which draws on literature, myth, songs, etc, is anti-sexism in education. By considering the progress of anti-sexist education, it is possible to see what conclusions might be drawn for the furtherance of multicultural, antiracist education.

How successful has the anti-sexist movement been? In short, it appears to be working. I want to argue that a contributing feature to the development of anti-sexist education during the 70s and 80s was the increasing numbers of feminists/women teachers who took issue with the ways girls were being discriminated against in the overt and hidden curriculum. Women teachers looked at girls' performance in a number of curriculum areas and began to research and investigate girls' poor performance, particularly in the 'male'-defined areas such as physics and mathematics (Kelly, 1987; Walden and Walkerdine, 1985; Walkerdine, 1988). Investigations extended to girls' use of the outside space, encouraging schools to look at how playgrounds and sports discourage girls participation (Ross et al., 1993). Feminist teachers, through force of numbers and commitment to change, were able to effect some changes in the school curriculum. Language and science offer two good examples of the impact and success of feminist ideas permeating the curriculum. The scrutiny of gender-specific language now makes it commonplace to adopt the gender-neutral terms as opposed to the gender-specific forms. It is no longer acceptable to use the word 'man' to include women in that generic sense.[1] Feminists debunked that bastion of curriculum 'neutrality', science education. Previously, science teachers had argued that science was not influenced by sexism or racism, that it was neutral. The work of Harding, (1986), Gill and Levidow (1987) and Peacock (1991) makes that claim laughable today.

It could be argued that feminists and women teachers who are conscious of the need to challenge sexism would also be conscious of promoting multiculturalism and antiracism. What then prevents many feminist teachers from seeing antiracism and antisexism as twin pillars of a common oppression?

The commonly shared experience of sexist discrimination put women in a position where, by drawing on those experiences, they better understood and appreciated the need to challenge and change existing discriminatory practices. However, White teachers are not positioned in the same way to racist exclusion, because they do not experience the exclusion themselves. The social class background of teachers will further determine what issues they feel best able to pursue, since social class interests enter experience and positionings too. So social class and social class loyalties have to be factors in this debate.

I am careful not to say, 'if you don't experience it you can't do anything about it' because it is not true. If it were, how could I explain antiracist campaigns, such as Teachers against Racism and Fascism, or the Anti-Nazi League? Clearly there are White people with insight and understanding into the outcomes of racist practices, and who can see similarities between forms of oppression. This is of particular importance because Black and other ethnic minorities make up such a tiny proportion of the British population, and therefore White educators will need to continue to play their part in developing antiracist education.

However, whatever loyalties most teachers feel, for most of them 'race' will not be a factor. Whereas the presence of Black staff within schools will inform and influence antiracist practice in ways which others cannot. The Swann Report argued that both White and Black children need to be offered positive Black role models if we are to begin to challenge racism in our society.

This point supports an argument for greater numbers of Black people in education who, because of their experience of racism, will be more likely to sustain a progressive attack against racism. My argument is that numbers are as important as political positions. This is so, even though not all Black people are antiracists, any more than all — or even most — women are feminists, and similarly, any more than all working class people are socialists. The point is that a critical mass is needed for policies and strategies to develop (Griffiths, 1995b).

Meanwhile, however, there are simply too few Black teachers. I therefore turn my attention to another group of people who are anxious to effect change to improve the educational chances of Black children: Black mothers. Black mothers have exhibited a fierce dedication to the advancement and education of their children. Education is something mothers strive ceaselessly to acquire for their children. Sacrifices made to obtain education have traditionally been seen as investments for the future. Doodsie stresses to her daughter Angel:

> Even if I have to go back on me knees and scrub in White people house and leave dis job here dat no payin' yours go be sure, too. But notice what ah tellin you. You not stupid. You could understand tings easier for man. Don' shame yourself an me. (Collins, 1987, p.103)

Education is seen as the only way out of poverty and hardship and the only legacy which poor parents can leave their children

> Ah have nothing to leave for you when ah dead. All ah have in you head so make de best of it (Collins 1987, p.101)

Mothers recognise that education offers children their only opportunity for social mobility.

The commitment to the betterment of their children was transferred 'back' across the Atlantic ('moral precepts') with parents during the 50s and 60s. Parents dutifully sent their children to school, now in the seat of the 'motherland', with the highest expectations. They were all the more shocked by the revelations in Bernard Coard's book (1971), which provided evidence that large numbers of West Indian children were being labelled Educationally Sub-Normal by the British education system. This book signalled to parents during the early 70s the degree to which their children were being discriminated against. Black children were disproportionately allocated to special education units, and removed from mainstream classroom activities (CCCS, 1989).

The level of the outcry and ensuing campaigns made it clear that parents recognised the situation as racist. The same practices they were encountering in the world of employment, housing and health care were also being found in the world of education (Bryant, Dadzie and Scafe, 1985; Williams, in James and Harris, 1993). A number of Supplementary/ Saturday schools were established as a result of parents' growing disillusion with the education system. The main concerns of supplementary schools were to provide a curriculum which reflected the Black experience of children and to help with basic literacy and numeracy.

The Survey

Why am I sure that Black parents know that it is racism which prevents their sons or daughters from progressing in schools? We have our experiences of living and working in a society which uses 'race' categories to 'exclude' groups of people from its resources. The aims of my questionnaire and interviews were rooted in this knowledge. My purpose was to find out about how Black families experience a Eurocentric education system. This is a question which is easier to formulate and ask from an 'active insider' position. Information was sought about: the age and circumstances of children; parents' opinions on school and racism; how best to prepare children for dealing with racism; and parents' recollections of their own experiences of racism in school.

One hundred and five questionnaires were posted out, using a strategy of 'network sampling'. This procedure follows that of other, earlier, social science inquiries into what were then little researched areas.[2] Parents known to me were asked to identify other parents with young children aged between three and a half and eight years old. Fifty-six questionnaires were completed and returned, yielding data on sixty-five children. Forty-three questionnaires were returned from within Greater London and the South East (Bedford, Croydon, Enfield, London, Luton and St Albans). The remaining thirteen came in from Manchester, Birmingham and Nottingham. Twenty one parents had received the major part of their schooling outside Britain (Barbados, Finland, Grenada, Jamaica, Ghana and Trinidad).

Ten face-to-face interviews were carried out to obtain fuller answers to certain questions. Five of these parents were from the London region, four of whom had received the majority of their education outside Britain. Three parents came from Nottingham, two of whom were schooled in Britain. Two parents were from St. Albans and Luton, one educated outside Britain, and the other having received only her college education in Britain.

The sixty five children were of the following ages and gender:

	Girls:	Boys:	Total
Children Ages 3 to 5	13	17	30
Children Ages 6 to 8	16	19	35

Answers to the Questionnaire

The answers to the questionnaire indicated the factors which influenced choices of school and included 'direct experience of schools' and their 'reputations'. In some cases, older siblings had attended the school.

> It was a known quantity, my oldest son had been to that school, and he was happy.

'Good' reputations were linked to the syllabus and to proximity to home and to minders. Eight parents mentioned the racial mix of children, and the need for a multicultural environment when selecting nurseries.

> Quality care and locality with a wide variety of activities and must be multicultural.

Children were prepared in a number of ways for what would be a Eurocentric curriculum. Thirty-one parents cited the home and the extended family, those in Britain and abroad (Barbados, Dominica, Finland, Jamaica, Trinidad and USA), as well as the child's immediate community, as factors which contributed to the child's preparation for school.

> It is important to develop a positive sense of self. I take her to the Caribbean each year — she has access to French and Spanish speakers.

Four (of the thirty-one parents) identified their own exclusive efforts in teaching their child: the alphabet, songs, rhymes and telling the child about school. As well as drawing on the wider community, parents provided 'books with positive images of Black people'. Personalised photo albums, music, posters, films, storytelling are all assembled to present the child with a sense of who they are and where they belong. This is put alongside advancing good academic skills.

Parents monitored the progress of their children. They visited school, read school reports, attended parents' meetings and read or looked at materials children brought home. If there were any causes for concern thay had no hesitation in approaching the school. Parents did not express any apprehension about approaching the school and teachers if they were dissatisfied with any aspect of schooling.

Parents actively promoted cultural distinctiveness. The skills and strategies called on to combat and develop children's cultural awareness, such as visiting relations and friends abroad or 'at home', are seen to be a crucial plank in developing children's cultural distinctiveness.

> We have been to French speaking countries and are going to France in two weeks time. I speak French and we read French books.

Responses to the Interviews

The ways that parents understand and discuss racism was illuminating. What became apparent during the face-to-face interviews was the parents' hesitation to name the act or experience of 'racism'. Instead, they talked around the issue. Yet they answered the questionnaire explicitly, with clear and unambiguous responses, especially when recalling the low expectation teachers had had of them.

> At the secondary phase at a careers meeting I was considered good secretarial material!! I have recently completed my second Masters.

I would suggest that perhaps one of the mechanisms by which racism works is to prevent people suffering from racism from naming the oppression. The opportunity to complete a written questionnaire reduced the discomfort and allowed parents to respond, leaving it to the author to have named the 'thing' that is racism.

Parents were sensitised to recognising stereotypes in books, materials and activities identified as carriers of racist ideas.

> I discuss with him what has happened each day. I spend periods of time in the room discussing materials and activities and meeting other parents and children in the class.

> My daughter came home with *Little Black Sambo* as her reading book. I was so vexed I made sure the next morning that they know how I felt about that damn book.

> Yes, if they [twins] speak of Blackness and colour of skin I let the school know I want it to be discussed and why.

Summary of results

To summarise, the intention of the research was to establish whether parents considered racism to be an issue in young children's education and, if so, what they felt they could do to counteract it.

Through talking and being active in children's school lives, parents can help children to promote cultural distinctiveness which, I believe, can afford some protection from the hurt of racism. Respondents to the questionnaire emphasised the need for cultural reinforcement through: talking to children about racism, and about colour and race related issues; offering children opportunities to become familiar with a wide range of positive experiences; helping children to become aware of their rights and opportunities; monitoring children's moods, behaviour and school work; teaching children about their family backgrounds; promoting pride in who and what they are; and reassuring children that difficult situations at schools, can be resolved by support from home. It is interesting that the responses above are in line with the work of James and Poussaint (1992), in the United States.

Conclusions

This exploratory study from the perspective of an insider has offered some preliminary answers to the question of why some Black children survive schooling in Britain more successfully than others. It has also highlighted some strategies that parents consider fundamental to supporting their children through a monocultural education system.

Furthermore, the chapter has highlighted the significance of insider researcher/writers. In an area which has received little academic scrutiny, Caribbean women's literature has served to provide some potent references to Black mothers' ambitions and aspirations for their children's educational success. Some familiarity with the literature, together with my gender and location within the African-Caribbean community, has positioned me at a pivotal intersection between race, class and gender. This makes it possible for me to ask questions about racism, and about the ambitions, values and attitudes that mothers have about their children and their interactions with schooling.

What has become very clear is that this is an unexplored area of study. It is one which is worth further exploration because it would help to give a voice to Black women concerned with bringing up and educating their family in Britain. Questions abound; many arise just from a critical look at the sample identified. For instance, the questionnaires were returned from London, the South East, Manchester, Birmingham and Nottingham: Are children afforded different strategies depending on where they go to school? Many parents had received the major part of their schooling outside Britain: would this factor have any bearing on parental attitudes and strategies available to support children? (I return to this question below.) There is need for much more research in the area and, especially, from an insider research perspective.

The research results identify, in a preliminary way, features which mothers operated in helping to support their children in schools. These have been briefly described here, but some of these features deserve greater attention. Firstly, what these data highlighted was that parents did in fact know about and monitor their children's progress in school with an eye to racist exclusion. They were willing to challenge educational malpractice and supplement their children's schooling.

> This school has a small ethnic intake. As one person it is difficult to take on a whole school with a predominantly White staff, from the outside. My son has a positive self-concept and this I feel is an essential asset in being part of an institution which I feel is in its infancy regarding the policy on racism. Why send him there in the first place? The high academic standard, which ultimately I want for my children, as I feel sure the family can 'cushion' or 'buffer' them to some point against racism.

Secondly, it seemed that mothers' own educational experiences might have some influence on their response to naming and acting on racist incidents and contexts. During interviews, six parents elaborated on their communications with schools.

> His teacher always had something bad to tell me ... But Martin[3] would always say it was not his fault and what he said always sounded reasonable to me. His work was not very good in that class. I certainly was not happy with what I was seeing and hearing. Martin was not happy ... I started to worry about it, but didn't know what to do. It was when he started fussing about going to school — he'd be complaining of stomach- and head-ache, bad leg ... That's when I changed him to the school down the road from here.

> They threatened to suspend ... Vincent, but I wasn't having any of it. ... He'd never been in any trouble before ... he's naughty but not wilful, and certainly not unmanageable. He did complain of one particular

159

teacher who just seem to be giving him a warm time. So I took a few days off work and went up to that school two days straight. I thought about moving him because I feel they are going to pick on him, but it seem to have sorted itself out ... Black boy children just seem to have so much trouble everywhere these days ... That was the last I heard of any suspension story. I still make sure I find out from Vincent what is happening, and I make it my business to read every piece of paper that come from his school.

Could these mothers' initial reluctance to act be due to their expectations of the education system? Mothers who appear to have received the majority of their schooling in Britain would seem not to have any 'misplaced' expectations. This is another area that would benefit from further investigations.

A theme of the chapter has been the similarities and differences between the antiracist and anti-sexist struggles. The anti-sexist movement has shown that change can be achieved, given enough action by those determined to achieve change. However, the tiny proportion of Black people in the education system, as teachers and as students, is significant. Certainly the study has highlighted the importance of the kind of home and school communication which would result in parents' ideas, ambitions and expectations to be taken on board in mainstream schools.

It could be argued that Supplementary/Saturday schools provide an example of where this symbiosis of parents and educators can come together to the benefit of the children's education. The relative success of these schools can be attributed to their cultural distinctiveness and the inclusion and involvement of parents. In such an environment the absence of a tension between culturally relevant material and learning appears to be reduced. Parents are visible and committed to the aims of these schools, and children enjoy success in an institution rooted in culture relevant to them. Here again, more research is needed.

It seems, on the evidence available, that mainstream schools have much to learn from the aims and practices of Supplementary/ Saturday schools, and their ability to make the best use of the energies of the mothers of their Black children. Ahfiwe is one such school:

We believe that a school such as Ahfiwe should promote a sense of oneness amongst our children, which should ... extend amongst the rest of the ... local community. It is our hope that our children will emerge from Ahfiwe feeling fully equipped with the power and ability to think and act critically to engage and combat the conflicts that they will face as Black people throughout their lives ... Areas covered will be: Black history/ makers of Black history. Countries of the Black world. Geography — different races of the world. Mineral resources/ food. Religion. Language. Way of life. (Ahfiwe, 1983)

Such schooling depends on the level of communication with the parents, and the willingness of both sides to make the considerable efforts involved. Such willingness is clearly demonstrated by the Black mothers I spoke to:

I want the best for my Makaba. She has a right to proper education. I know I have to do a lot more than most White mothers. So I will just have to do it.

Notes

1. Witness how usual it is for traditional publishers and Universities to have such language policies nowadays.
2. See, for instance, the classic study of childminders (Jackson, 1979).
3. All names have been changed.

Chapter 10

Some ethical dilemmas in field work:
feminist and antiracist methodologies

Mehreen Mirza

Introduction

This chapter discusses some of the methodological and ethical predica-
ments I faced as a British South Asian woman[1] conducting research on
other South Asian females, as part of doctoral research. These methodological and ethical dilemmas arise from attempting to translate seemingly
'lofty and intimidating' (Scanlon, 1993) feminist[2] and antiracist epistemological principles into practice, in effect conducting 'research as praxis'
(Lather, 1986), such that there is no division between theory and practice.
I seek to illustrate 'the myriad of complexities that lie behind the intention
to or the assertion of doing antiracist, feminist research' (Neal, 1995).

The chapter briefly states the aims of the research, provides a brief
discussion of the feminist and antiracist epistemological position it sought

to adopt, and then discusses the methodological and ethical dilemmas that arose during the fieldwork, primarily in the research relationship, focusing in particular on: access to a sample population, 'placing' of interviewers, 'matching' of interviewers and interviewees and 'reciprocity' in interviews.

The research

The research is an exploratory piece of work with the general aim of examining South Asian girls and women's experiences of education in 'non-traditional' areas[3]: in school, further education and higher education settings in the North West of England. The research sought to gain an insight into their experiences and therefore does not claim to provide data which is representative or transferable to other situations. In order to obtain as broad a range of experiences as possible, the research focused on Year 9 and Year 11 students in school; first and second year 'A'-level and BTEC students at further education colleges, and sub-degree (HND); first degree and postgraduate students at higher education institutions, studying non-traditional subject areas. A range of methods was employed, which included questionnaires and interviews. However the predominant method was that of interviewing, which ranged from the structured, through the semi-structured to the unstructured. In total, 75 interviews were conducted.

Methods, in and of themselves, are neutral; it is how they are used which is the issue. I chose to pursue a qualitative research methodology in order to 'understand the ... women's lives from their own perspectives' (Brah and Shaw, 1992, p.53). I felt that the interview technique would best allow social processes to be examined and questions of 'how' and 'why' to be answered. Thus the 'methodology allows respondents to discuss their experiences, beliefs and values, and the social meaning they attach to a given phenomenon in a relaxed and informal atmosphere' (*ibid* p.53). This was especially important here, as I sought to explore sensitive issues such as gender, 'race', culture and religion, as well as the area of 'non-traditional subjects', which can be difficult. Interviewing enables respondents to move beyond answering the questions asked, to raising other issues and concerns which the researcher might not have considered or seen as relevant, thus providing 'considerable opportunity for respondents to control the interview and hence to dictate the content and form of the data' (Brannen, 1988, p.555). All but one of the interviews were tape-recorded, with the permission of the respondents, as the verbal accounts were ultimately the only source of data and thus had to be accurate.

Feminist and antiracist research

Research by its very nature is inherently political and it is about the nature of power as well as access to power. The academy has been dominated by White middle-class and/or male researchers, whose political values and commitments have influenced social research, leading it to be pre-dominately Eurocentric, bourgeois and patriarchal in its agenda. This agenda has been informed by the dominant groups, such that the marginal, the powerless and the oppressed have been the excessive object of study. The significance is that South Asian females in the British context, by virtue of their ethnicity/'race' and gender, can be conceived of as power-less, oppressed and marginal in society, in relation to the dominant groups. Antiracist and feminist research differ from one another in focus, but they are often placed together, as in this research, because of 'their shared rejection of objective, apolitical, scientific research' (Neal, 1995, p.3). What is crucial in determining the epistemological and methodological approach is that it should avoid the conventional 'view from nowhere' stance of White western epistemology.

There is no one feminist methodology or epistemological approach. There are, however, the following shared assumptions. First, it should address women's lives and experience in their own terms and ground theory in the actual experiences of women. Second, it should promote an interactional methodology in order to end the exploitation of women as research objects. Third, research on women should provide the women studied with explanations that could be used to improve their life situations, such that they do not become objectified. Finally, the researcher is central to the research and her feelings should be central to the process.[4]

These assumptions lead to a particular set of principles by which to conduct feminist research; that is, an overt and political commitment to the researched, as well as a commitment to doing non-hierarchical, reciprocal, negotiated, emancipatory and subjective research which would be about women, for women and conducted from within women's perspectives, such that it prioritises the participants' needs over and above that of the need to collect data.

The convergence between racist ideologies and the theories of 'race/ethnic' relations sociology has resulted in researchers focusing not on the 'State and its functionaries' (Goldberg, 1993) or even on 'racial' inequality and the racist nature and the structure of the social system, but on the Black communities themselves. These communities have been constructed as problematic vis-à-vis the White middle-class 'norm'. Black women and girls are often excluded from studies on work which seek to understand 'normal' women, and come into focus only when the research shifts to considering devalued groups, reproducing many cultural and racial stereotypes. For instance, young African-Caribbean women come into focus as the assumed problematic 'teenage mothers' and South Asian females come into view on the issue of 'arranged marriages' (Brah and Minhas, 1985; Lawrence, 1982; Phoenix, 1994a, 1994b). Further, young Black people, and particularly young Asian women are seen to be 'caught between two cultures', struggling to deal with the alleged freedom of the 'host' society and the traditional, authoritarian nature of their parents' culture (Connolly, 1993; Lawrence, 1982; Mac an Ghaill, 1988 and 1989; Neal, 1995). Indeed, these concerns can be seen in the titles of various studies conducted: 'The Second Generation ... Punjabi or English' (Thompson, 1974 cited in Lawrence 1982, p.122) and 'The silent cry: second generation Bradford Muslim women speak' (Mirza, 1989).

I sought to pursue antiracist research, but antiracist principles are problematic to define. However it can be argued that, at a basic level, research is antiracist if it problematises and challenges racism. At a more complex level, antiracist research can be judged on its ability to contribute towards specific antiracist struggles as well as its ability to make sense of the origins and nature of specific racist social processes and practices. Further, it is contended that antiracist research should end the division between theory and practice and it should promote praxis. It should also be informed by the principles of social justice, equality and participatory democracy to which the researchers should be committed (Ben-Tovim et al., 1986; Connolly, 1993; Lather, 1986; Troyna and Carrington, 1993).

It follows that the praxis demands that antiracist (and anti-sexist research) should analyse institutional racism (and sexism) rather than study Black people (and women). Thus there is no one way to judge the validity of research, but it should not wittingly or unwittingly contribute to further racist/sexist/bourgeois oppression or interpretation.

It is argued that feminist methodology has rejected patriarchal assumptions in social science research but has reproduced racist assumptions (Marshall, 1994) and antiracist research has often neglected issues of gender (Christian, 1989, p.21). Indeed, it is frequently argued that feminism fails to take into account the complex ways in which gender inequalities interrelate with class and race oppression. Thus Black and White feminists are increasingly seeking a methodology which is able to address the interlocking nature of oppression based on 'race', class and gender.

Black feminist standpoint epistemology[5] stems from the desire to understand the position of Black women and their experience of double subjectivity. Collins (1990) argues that this double subjectivity can be viewed as their 'outsider within status'. That is, the ability to be both inside and outside of that which they research, such that they understand both. Indeed it enables a process of self-actualisation whereby the Black woman as researcher or researched is an 'active subject', thus counteracting the trend of pathologisation and dehumanisation in academic research.

Collins (1991) outlines four assumptions which underpin Black feminist epistemology: firstly that the content of thought (in terms of structure and theme) cannot be separated from the historical and material conditions which shape the lives it produces. Thus Black feminist standpoint can only be produced by Black women. Secondly, there is an assumption that Black women as a group will share certain commonalties. However, thirdly, there are diversities between Black women on the basis of class, region, age, and sexual orientation. Finally, there is a recognition that even though a Black women's standpoint might exist, it may not be apparent to all Black women.

Beyond these assumptions, there are at least four key themes within this Black feminist standpoint. Firstly, it promotes 'self-definition' by Black women which seeks to reject externally created stereotypical images of Black women. Secondly, it seeks 'self-valuation' such that it overcomes external definitions and replaces them with 'authentic Black female images'. Self-definition and self-valuation overcome the dehumanising and objectifying process of being viewed as 'other'. Thirdly, the interlocking nature of 'race', gender, and class oppression is acknowledged. Black women can see more clearly the nature of oppression so that:

unlike White women, they have no illusions that their Whiteness will negate female subordination, and unlike Black men, they can not use a questionable appeal to manhood to neutralise the stigma of being Black. (Collins, 1991, p.41)

By engaging in the multiple nature of oppression and the larger matrix of domination, individuals are able to see that 'oppression is complex and contradictory such that no one is ever either oppressor/oppressed' (Collins, 1990, p.229), but may be 'an oppressor, a member of an oppressed group, or simultaneously oppressor and oppressed' (Collins, 1990, p.225). Thus the value of this approach lies in seeking to understand the interconnectedness but also enables a consideration of the specificity of each variable as it arises. The fourth, and final, key theme is the recognition that culture is not static, but created and modified through material conditions.

As a South Asian woman researcher I was in the double position of being a member of the White Western academy, which traditionally oppresses and marginalises through racism the communities from which she comes. This leads to the difficulties of trying to 'both step out of and also draw on one's subjective awareness of the social, economic and political subordination of one's community' (Marshall, 1994, p.109).

The three approaches outlined above, feminist, antiracist, and Black feminist research, which I have endeavoured to pursue, share the common principles of equity, non-hierarchy, negotiation, emancipation, subjectivity and reciprocity in the research process.

Doing antiracist and feminist research

Research is political and it is also infused by ethical considerations. This section will discuss the methodological and ethical dilemmas confronted when seeking to implement feminist and antiracist epistemological principles.

Access to a sample population

As with all social and educational research, the issue of gate-keepers arose. Headteachers and Principals had given access to their educational institutions, but the next stage of negotiation was with the deputy heads or heads of relevant departments, who acted as 'gatekeepers' to the students. A fine balance had to be maintained between pursuing research objectives and meeting the needs of the institutions, especially since access was a privilege, not a right. My bargaining position rested on the potential end findings, which could be of benefit to the establishments with regard to their teaching and equal opportunities work.

When I made contact with potential respondents at school level (in person or by letter of introduction), I told them about the aims of the research and their right not to participate in any stage of the research. I also said that I would like to interview some of them, and why. Those who agreed to be interviewed were asked to indicate when they would be available for interview, for instance: before school, during lunchtime or after school. At this stage I began to lose my pool of school-age respondents. It is impossible to know exactly why a person or group of people choose not to take part in research, but there were some reasons which became fairly apparent on closer examination. It transpired that parents discouraged any after-school activity. It was also considered impossible for me to interview the students in their own homes, as it was seen by the students to be an unacceptable and potentially threatening situation. (This is explored further below.) Consequently, finding a suitable time to interview students, where the schools concerned would not allow access during class-time, became problematic.

Thus my desire for a systematic representative sample fell by the wayside. In the end I pursued an 'opportunistic' snow-ball sampling approach, which was obviously self-selecting. Finding the 'opportunities' was difficult, and this began to cause me considerable concern.

Often research is of marginal importance to the researched, who therefore decide on making alternative, perhaps better, use of their time. It is suspected that this particular group of students could see no obvious benefit. The use of 'traditional' methods, especially evoking the name of the university and the university's interest, may not be — and was not — successful, as it has different connotations. That is, we need to avoid assuming that 'institutions which give us status and credibility in the eyes of White women will necessarily do so in the eyes of Black women' (Edwards, 1990, p.485). In addition, the subject areas I was covering (non-traditional subject areas, equal opportunities, racism and sexism) were not felt by the respondents to be important. My position as a young, female researcher carried no status and thus I could not make the issues important to the respondents. The South Asian women/girls were concerned about the research process, confidentiality and the motivations of the research: 'Why was I doing this, who was funding it, who would the report be written for, what angle was I coming from?' as well as 'what was the purpose of all these questions?'. The wariness was understandable.

But the nature of the community itself hinders access; for instance:

Asian women are a very difficult group to study and gain easy access to, some of whom belong to very close knit groups who have and portray a very strong sense of belonging and security in which their cultural identity is reinforced as essential to the well-being of the society, the culture and the individuals. Outsiders who do not identify with the group will be viewed with suspicion and seen as a threat to which they may disturb / affect the pattern of harmony that exists in the community. Members of the community will question what it is the outsiders want and how they may affect the daily lives of the individuals who live in the community. (Bhopal, 1994, p.4)

Importantly, I had no wider links with the South Asian community in the North West of England. I had moved there in order to work and study. In seeking to do the research and make contact with the respondents, I felt as though I were being 'parachuted in' (Jeffers, 1991 cited in Brar, 1992) which also led to difficulties.

Appearance

Presentation of self is crucial in research and affects both the process of negotiation to obtain potential respondents and the actual interview process itself. Much of the discussion on the nature of appearance (dress and physical appearance) focuses on the issue as it arises when interviewing men (Carol Smart, 1984 cited in Neal 1995, p.8). However it became a dilemma for me even though I was researching predominately women.

My dilemma was that I needed to dress for three separate audiences: the potential respondents and subsequent interviewees, the educational gate-keepers and educational staff (especially in school settings) and for my employers. Each had distinct requirements, but it was critical that I should get it right. Dress, especially in relation to girl students in schools, is crucial in 'gaining access to people ... and ultimately getting their trust

... [and] gaining acceptance from the girls' (Measor, 1985, p.61), and ultimately it determines the data obtained. In order to meet with the educational gate-keepers, to gain access to the educational establishments (especially schools) and to look as though I belonged there, I needed to present an image that was in keeping with that of a teacher; that is, fairly smart, conservative and respectable. On the other hand, to fit in with the students I needed something less formal that would enable me to gain access to their world and achieve some level of rapport in order to conduct the research, and which, importantly, would not cause offence or upset their sensibilities. For my employers, fairly casual wear was acceptable. My dilemma arose as I was often required to meet with all three on the same day. But it was most acute in the field. That is, I needed to wear 'teacher-like' clothes in order to gain access to the schools and appear at the very least as though I was a 'bona fide' researcher (Smart, 1984, p.153 in Neal, 1995, p.8), while still appearing suitable to meet the respondents.

I decided that a smart pair of trousers and blouse would do. However, in the actual interviewing situation it became apparent that my garb and the amount of make-up I wore was not acceptable, as the respondents commented negatively upon them. They would have found a more 'traditional' South Asian form of dress more acceptable (such as *shalwar kameez*), to judge by comments like: 'My parents wouldn't let me wear that' and 'That outfit is indecent'. However, a traditional form of dress would not have given me access to the school in quite the same way; as one gate-keeper commented: 'You're not like the students here. You're so Western. You're like one of us'. My compromise suited no-one. Others (see for example, Green et al., 1993) have resolved the problem by carrying a change of clothing. However as I did not have my own means of transport at the time, it was impossible to juggle a bag full of alternative clothing, a tape-recorder, interview schedules, purse, personal alarm etc.

As someone who has had cropped hair for a number of years, I realised that the length of my hair could cause a problem by not being seen as 'acceptable' by the South Asian girls/women I sought to interview. Therefore, I grew it as long as I could, that is shoulder length and able to be tied back, but it still proved to be unacceptable. It still drew attention as being 'different' (indeed of all the interviewees I met, only two had short hair). Again it was commented upon negatively, 'Asian girls aren't allowed/supposed to have short hair'. Or I was questioned about my hair:

Respondent:	Did your mum and dad not mind you cutting your hair?
MM:	No. Would you want your hair cut?
Respondent:	Well I was asking my mum if I could get a perm and she goes 'Well you ask your dad and you take your dad to the hairdresser' and that means 'No, your dad would never let you. Your dad'll never say yeah.'

While these comments can be considered amusing, I feel that they seriously affected the level of rapport I was able to achieve with the students (discussed below).

Identity

More critically, I became aware that in order to cope with all the different people I was required to deal with, I was developing 'shifting identities', not only through my mode of dress but through my actual behaviour. Lois Weis notes that:

> The fact that people define us in certain ways does have an effect on us, whether positive or negative. It is therefore important that researchers know who they are, before entering the field because others will define you as they see fit. (1992, p.50)

Further she argues that :

> One is what others define you to be in these settings and this definition is likely to be more removed from one's real self the further removed from one's original culture when doing fieldwork. (1992, p.50)

Adelman echoes this when he suggests that, in order to overcome misrepresentation, the researcher should be a competent member of the culture he/she is writing about (1985, p.43). The development of my shifting and multiple identities made me uncomfortable. Although I realise that we all possess multiple identities, this particular creation made me question whether I was a competent member of the South Asian community, as well as questioning who I was.

Placing

This section discusses the issue of 'matching of interviewer and inter-viewee' and the issue of 'placing' by interviewees of the interviewer as the two are closely intertwined. At the start of the research, there was an underlying assumption that as a woman of South Asian origin I would be able to make contacts within the South Asian community simply because I was South Asian. In other words, the particular combination of my gender and 'race' would give me a passport into the community. How-ever, as already indicated, it was not quite so simple.

Finch (1984) discusses the critical need for 'placing' to occur when women interview women. She argues that:

> One's identity as a woman therefore provides the entree into the interview situation ... The interviewer has to be prepared to expose herself to being 'placed' as a woman and to establish that she is willing to be treated accordingly. (1984, pp.79-80)

She goes on to say that 'Once these identifications are made, it does indeed seem the easiest thing in the world to get women to talk to you' (1984, p.80). Finch found that because the women perceived her to be 'one of them' (1984, p.79) they 'became warm and eager to talk' (p.79). The critical category for 'placing' here is gender, followed by particularistic others such as marriage, motherhood, or mother-in-law-hood. I assumed that my critical categories would be shared-gender and shared-'race'.

As I went into the field to obtain a sample and subsequently began interviewing, I realised that a superficial placing on the basis of shared gender and shared 'race' is simply not enough, especially when one is seeking to 'create shared meanings'. Indeed these factors, together with my social class, age, and background became increasingly significant, and thus led to a dynamic situation of 'shifting similarities and differences and hence shifting sympathies' (Phoenix, 1994a, p.58). In focusing on the similarities between myself and the respondents, in order to conduct ethically sound and methodologically honest research which would pro-vide 'good' data, I found that the differences between us became greater, to a point where a respondent felt it necessary at the end of an interview to ask: 'You are Asian, aren't you?' Thus, in the field, same-sex and same-'race' interviewing was proving to be problematic.

Much of the discussion between the respondents and myself which suggested my 'non-placing', occurred before and after the 'formal interview' when the tape recorder was switched off. Nevertheless, it is possible to surmise a number of reasons why I was not placed, including, for example, the fact that I was not from the North West of England. This was significant in two ways. Firstly, I was frequently asked who I was related to in the area, to which I would respond, no-one as far as I was aware. This seemed to give the respondents the impression that I was detached from the community, since the remark attracted comments like: 'Don't your parents mind?' Secondly, it is increasingly recognised that how people, especially South Asian women/girls, experience their ethnicity is in part dependent upon their location (Bhachu, 1991). The South Asian community in the North West is fairly working-class and conservative in nature (Ali, 1992), which does not quite reflect my experience as I come from a large conurbation. For instance one respondent commented:

I mean in the North, I think people are still very ... well I'm talking about my experience this is, well it's a bit of a closed community thing. It's restricted ... But if you go further down South the family becomes more Western ... They're totally different to what we are like. Very.

Moreover, I lived on my own, which was uncommon and socially disapproved of by 'the community', as indicated by the respondent who suggested that:

They wouldn't mix with my dad ... They wouldn't exactly come up to me and say, 'You're like this and you're like that'. They'd probably smile in front of my face, but when it came to talking to my dad, they'd probably look down on him and because Asians are supposed to respect their parents. Anyway, you wouldn't do that kind of stuff.

Additionally, I was still relatively young. My professional status as a researcher, associated with a university, carried very little weight. I was thus perceived as 'statusless'. Obviously I was not disrupting their community as an anthropologist might do, but I was disrupting their understanding of what a South Asian woman ought to be and the kind of work that she should do. The girls/women I wished to approach/interview were wary of me and were not prepared to be interviewed in their homes becauses I was seen as a 'threat' as I could not be 'placed' within their or their family's understanding of the social world. This was summed up for me by one interviewee who said, 'my mother- in-law would not like you'. On enquiry, it transpired that this meant I would be seen as a 'threat' because I would be considered 'abnormal/deviant' within their social circle. My perceived 'deviancy' was due to my marital status, appearance, demeanour, and the fact that I was doing the research which meant that I could not be 'one of them'.

Despite our mutual desire to place one another, our inability to do so successfully often meant that during interviews the respondents would defend themselves, as though my very presence was an implicit criticism of their lives and their social world. This caused me much discomfort and ethical concern, when women would excuse their religious beliefs in an apologetic manner when they needed to go to pray, etc., , as though they felt they were not quite right. This process of placing created me as 'other' as opposed to marginal (which I had been prepared for and accepted). Being perceived of as 'other' by the wider society is something that I have come to accept; to be constructed as 'other' within what one assumes to be one's own culture/society is something else.

In discussions about the career roles that South Asian women/girls could take, we would discuss the then current soap opera 'Family Pride'. Regardless of its merits or demerits as a soap, it had several female characters in professional roles. The respondents saw these roles as totally unrealistic and inapplicable to their own lives and consigned them to fantasy land. When I challenged this by saying that surely I was not fantasy, it was again emphasised that maybe where I came from that was possible, but not for them. Again I was the 'other'.

I hasten to add that there were cases of successful placing, but these involved a shared 'culture', class, life-style and aspirations as well as shared gender and race.

The advantage of not being placed was that:

Such 'placings' and assumptions may be particularistic, but they can also give researchers pointers to the ways in which groups of people construct and make sense of their lives in circumstances other than the interview itself' (Edwards, 1993, p.195).

Further, respondents would often say in response to a question 'Well *you* probably don't know this, but Asians'... or 'In *our* culture...'. Thus I felt that I had achieved the 'insider/outsider' position I had sought, although perhaps rather more of the outsider than insider. It enabled me to get more 'objective' data, where assumptions were not made (see Rhodes, 1994): Thus I disrupted any sense of the familiar and played the role of the stranger within (Collins, 1990). Indeed I felt that it was positive because it has been reported that Black people will not necessarily 'talk openly about their experiences and opinions' with other Black people, especially Black researchers (Rhodes, 1994, p.551).

On the other hand, the most negative aspect, over and above lack of rapport and access to a sample population, was that the personal cost was high. It raised questions of: Who was I? What was I? Why didn't I belong? This always made me feel uncomfortable, as it made me wonder how respondents perceived me: was I viewed as an honorary White person? This notion was disturbing.

The interview situation

A feminist approach to research seeks one based on a non-hierarchical, non-exploitative, reciprocal and shared-sex basis, with the potential to lead to friendship (Bergen, 1993; Edwards, 1993; Finch, 1984; Oakley, 1981). One of the preferred methods is interviewing. In these circumstances the interview is conceived of as a...

> collaborative interactional process in which the 'work' consists of the construction of meanings, with reciprocal inputs from researcher and researched, arriving at agreed conclusions on interpretation of the content, or data of the research. (Holland and Ramazanoglu, 1994, p.135)

This spirit of equality involves the use of reciprocity and self-disclosure, as it overcomes inhibitions on the part of the interviewee and places the researcher and researched on a par.

Finch argues that this is possible due to a cultural affinity between women interviewers and the women they are interviewing, because they 'share a subordinate structural position by virtue of their gender' (Finch, 1984, p.76). Edwards argues that the effects of self-disclosure can be firstly, to allow research 'rules' to be broken; and secondly to promote the sense of identification the women looked for with the researcher: 'All the women indicated at least some feelings or experiences that we shared' (Edwards, 1993, p.192). Finally, it enables women to make links between shared experiences and to create a sense of solidarity with those in the same situation.

Earlier discussions highlighted the value of 'self-disclosure'. I would try to do this at opportune moments, before, during and after the interview in my attempt to establish a conversational style. It became apparent, however, that this was not always welcome, as it interrupted the women's own flow of thought. Moreover, self-disclosure on my part to enable rapport actually created further distance. That is, I became more 'alien' and 'unplaceable'. Thus, when asked my opinions on a subject, I initially provided as honest an answer as I could. However, this would often caused surprise and elicit further questions, until, probing further into my background in an attempt to explain/explore my response, the respondents would say 'Ah, that explains it!' (my peculiar opinion) and we were able to carry on. Becoming an interviewee became an uncomfortable position because of the continual challenges to my identity, and I began to develop an increasingly 'uneasy and ironic adoption of a traditional, 'malestream' academic persona, presenting myself as neutral, rational and objective' (Neal, 1995, p.8). This could be seen as unethical and the antithesis of good feminist praxis (Ball, 1992). However I consider it a realistic response to the 'messiness' of real research as I felt that, like the respondents, I had a right to present a public account of myself and maintain some privacy.

Pay-back time

Seeking to do more than just respond to questions, in an attempt at reciprocity so as to 'pay back' the respondents for their time and information, proved problematic and generated further dilemmas. For instance, the respondents did not express any interest in reciprocity and appeared to want nothing from me. Indeed they would often say 'Why? What for?' 'That's silly!' and 'There's no need, you need my help and I'm happy to give it you'. In effect it was a favour to me, a complete stranger. The occasional expression of reciprococity often took the form of straightforward requests in exchange for their time and information, such as asking advice on the best type of video-camera to purchase or the nearest

Asian women's photography club, or on negotiating the tricky world —
of GCSE and A-level options, or completing UCAS forms — in other
words of utilising my 'expertise'. For others, there was no such obvious
service I could offer. Some of the respondents, flatteringly, credited me
with more power than I had, requesting that I set up a course for South
Asian women in the subject areas that they were interested in. My
response that I could only recommend it as a policy option was met with
disappointment.

Others caused me considerable concern in the manner in which they
sought 'pay-back'. For instance, I was perceived as a suitable person to
intervene on behalf of the respondent in a marriage proposal. I was not
prepared to do so, as I felt that it was inappropriate, but the respondent
felt that I should — as I could — 'help'. Another, a year after an interview,
called to say that she had not passed all her 'A'- levels and was keen to
do a law degree, and insisted that I use my contacts to ensure her a place
on a suitable course. I could not possibly do so, but it was expected that
I would, in return for the information she had provided.

Respondents were not the only ones to perceive me in this way.
Gate-keepers often shared the perception of me as a professional South
Asian woman. For instance, one gate-keeper sought my aid in intervening
between the school and a set of parents who were refusing to let their
daughters come to school. It was felt that I could persuade the parents to
return their daughters to school. The school expected this in return for
having allowed me access. I declined as best I could, without appearing
unhelpful and endangering access.

Whose agenda?

I wanted to pursue interviews in a spirit of reciprocity but in the case of
this research this often proved self-deluding because the researcher
constructs the research problem, constructs the questions, seeks the
relationship with respondents and ultimately determines what happens to
the material created. Ultimately 'What is in it for them is never what is in
it for you. Even if they were interested it is usually not for the *knowledge*
of it' (Glucksmann, 1994, p.154 original emphasis).

The research study, like many others, produced harrowing accounts of
experiences that some of the South Asian women/girls I interviewed were
experiencing, or had experienced. I recognised that, despite my good

intentions, I was not really in a position to 'help' and should and did as Brannen suggests, remain 'silent yet empathetic [which] is hard and yet it may be all that the individual can offer in the circumstances' (1988, p.560). Despite the reciprocal approach, it did not feel appropriate to intervene in circumstances where I, as an outsider, perceived the respondents' circumstances to be oppressive, but the respondents did not. The effects of such revelations were disturbing to me but may have been far more traumatic for the respondent, such that after an interview 'the subject may be left with her emotional life in pieces and no-one to help put them back together — a situation that Clark and Haldane have graphically termed the 'scientific equivalent of slash and burn agriculture" (Clark and Haldane, 1990, p.143 cited in Edwards, 1993, p.192-3). Is it ethically acceptable to have done this?

Conclusion

The aim of this chapter has been to explore the complexities of attempting to operationalise antiracist and feminist epistemological and methodological principles into practice in a particular situation (and makes no claims to be representative). It illustrates how problematic research praxis can be, even in a 'best case' situation where the researched and researcher are matched on the basis of 'race' and gender. My experience indicates that 'placing' and successful reciprocal relationships are dependent upon much more than a shared gender and 'race'. The 'failure' in achieving reciprocity/rapport demonstrates the danger of creating a 'false-equality' trap (Gelsthorpe, 1992) where none exists. Indeed, the role of the 'stranger' is a valid and valuable one (Collins, 1990; Cotterill, 1992) and should not be dismissed.

The chapter has primarily addressed issues concerned with feminist research praxis, as they were the ones which were often most pertinent, although their manifestation was in some ways racialised and culture-specific. My intention was to pursue antiracist praxis and focus on 'White institutions and White discourses' (Neal, 1995) but that was not possible. However in shifting the gaze to the South Asian women/girls themselves, I sought to provide a means by which they could voice their opinions and present their experiences in a manner which did not pathologise them and, importantly, did not add feed into the stereotypes. I wanted to ensure that in making visible and recording the experiences of this group, I did not fall into the trap of informing the powerful about an oppressed group (1994; Neal, 1995; Stacey, 1988). This is especially significant in relation to Black women whose relationship with the state is one of oppression (Carby, 1982; Bryant et al., 1985; Mama, 1989; Parmar, 1982). Hence my desire to pursue an approach that would challenge existing perceptions, and address the priorities of Black women, so that the research could be used to improve the position of Black women in Britain. (Marshall, 1994, p.120). Further, it is a recognition that when viewed by the state, I am one of the researched and so acknowledging 'my subordination as a Black woman whilst recognising my privileged position in relation to other women in regard to class, sexuality, age and ability. Like other feminists I share the common dilemma of reconciling my personal life and my political goals' (Marshall, 1994, p.122-3).

Despite difficulties I maintain a commitment to 'an antiracist socialist feminist understanding of the sources of oppression' (Ball, 1992, p.12), with its attendant principles (as discussed earlier). The value of conducting research on an 'insider/outsider' basis is great, even if, in my case, I was ultimately more 'outsider' than 'insider'. This recognition leads me to continually question and deconstruct notions of what it means to be an 'insider' and 'outsider', and, especially, to question and deconstruct the concept 'South Asian female', in order to overcome essentialist perspectives of South Asian womanhood.

Notes

1. The term 'South Asian' is used to refer to those who define their heritage and/or ethnic origins as originating from the South Asian sub-continent, which incorporates Bangladesh, India and Pakistan. The term is used merely for convenience. The term 'woman' is also problematic, since the concept 'woman' and the experience of being a woman is and must be 'ontologically fractured and complex' (Stanley and Wise, 1990, p.22).

2. Although the concept 'feminism' is used, it is recognised to be problematic. It is assumed to be 'open and 'generic' yet it is increasingly argued that it is implicitly White in its concerns and focus (hooks, 1984; Kishwar, 1994; Stanley and Wise, 1993).

3. 'Non-traditional' subject areas are those academic disciplines and related career areas that are considered 'non-traditional' for females in Western Europe and North America such as architecture, engineering etc.

4. See, for example, Du Bois, 1983; Fonow and Cook, 1991; Duelli Klein, 1983; Edwards, 1993; Finch, 1984; Harding, 1986; 1987 and 1991; Herbert, 1993; Mies, 1983; Oakley, 1981; Ollenburger and Moore, 1992; Renzetti and Lee, 1993; Stanley and Wise 1993, for more detailed discussions of the nature and complexity of feminist epistemology and methodology, than I able to provide here.

5. See Harding, 1986 and 1991 for detailed discussions of feminist standpoint epistemology.

References

Aboud, F. (1988) *Children and Prejudice*, Oxford, Basil Blackwell

Adelman C. (1985) 'Who are you? Some problems of ethnographer culture shock' in R. G. Burgess (Ed) *Field Methods in the Study of Education*, Lewes, Falmer Press

Ahfiwe Saturday School (1983) *Aims and Objectives*, London, Ahfiwe Saturday School

Ali, Y. (1992) 'Muslim women and the politics of ethnicity and culture in Northern England', in G. Shagal and N. Yuval-Davis (Eds), *Refusing holy orders*, London, Virago Press

Alleyne, M. (1988) *Roots of Jamaican Culture*, London, Pluto

Amos, Valerie and Parmar Pratibha (1981) 'Resistance and responses: black girls in Britain' in A. McRobbie and T. McCabe (Eds) *An Adventure Story for Girls: Feminist Perspectives on Young Women*, London, Routledge and Kegan Paul

Amos, Valerie and Parmar, Pratibha (1984) 'Challenging Imperial Feminism' in *Feminist Review (Special issue: Many Voices One Chant, Black Feminist Perspectives)*, 17, Autumn

Anderson, K., Armitage, S., Jack, D. and Wittner, J. (1990) 'Beginning Where We Are: Feminist Methodology in Oral History' in J. McCarl Nielsen (ed) *Feminist Research Methods*, Colorado, Westview Press

Anderson, G. L. and Herr, K. (1994) 'The micropolitics of student voices: moving from diversity of bodies to diversity of voices in schools' in C. Marshall (ed) *The New Politics of Race and Gender,* London, Falmer Press

Anthias, F. and Yuval-Davis, N. (1992) *Racialised Boundaries: race, nation, gender, colour, class and the anti-racist struggle*, London, Routledge

Anwar, M. (1979) *The Myth of Return,* London, Heinemann

Apple, Michael (1977) 'Ivan Illich and Deschooling Society' in M. Young and G. Whitty (eds) *Society, State and Schooling*, Lewes, Falmer Press

Arnot, Madeleine (1991) 'Equality and Democracy: a decade of struggle over education' in *British Journal of Sociology of Education*, 12, 4, 447-467

Asher, S. R. and Gottman, J. M. (eds) (1981) *The Development of Children's Friendships*, Cambridge, Cambridge University Press

Asian Times, Campaign forces Home Office climb-down, 3 December 1994

Atkinson, P. (1983) 'The Reproduction of Professional Community', in: R. Dingwall and P. Lewis (eds) *Sociology of the Professions*, London, Macmillan.

Atkinson, D. (1994) *Radical Urban Solutions: Urban Renaissance for City Schools and Communities*, London, Cassell

Back, Les (1990) *Racist Name-Calling and Developing Anti-Racist Initiatives in Youth Work*, Research Paper in Ethnic Relations No.14, Coventry, Centre for Research in Ethnic Relations, University of Warwick

Back, Les (1991) 'Social Context and Racist Name-Calling: An Ethnographic Perspective on Racist Talk within a South London Adolescent Community' *European Journal of Intercultural Studies* 1, 19-38

Back, Les (1993) 'Race, identity and nation within an adolescent community in South London' *New Community* 19, 217-233

Back, Les (1994) The White Negro revisited, in A. Cornwall and N. Lindisfarne (eds) *Dislocating Masculinity, Comparative Ethnographies*. London, Routledge

Back, Les and Solomos, John (1992) *Doing Research, Writing Politics.* Paper presented to Race and Research Workshop, Birkbeck College, University of London

Ball, D. (1979) Self and identity in the context of deviance: the case of criminal abortion in M. Wilson (ed) *Social and Educational Research in Action,* Milton Keynes, Open University Press

Ball, Stephen (1985) 'Interviewing Pupils' in Burgess, R. (ed) *Strategies of Qualitative Research*, Barcombe, Falmer Press

Ball, Stephen (1987) *The Micro-Politics of the School. Towards a Theory of School Organization*, London, Methuen

Ball, Wendy (1991) 'The ethics and politics of doing anti-racist research in education: key debates and dilemmas', *European Journal of Intercultural Studies*, 2 (1) 35-49

Ball, Wendy (1992) 'Critical social research, adult education and antiracist feminist praxis' *Studies in the Education of Adults*, 24 (1) April, 1-25

Ball, Wendy (1994) 'Racial equality policies and the 'everyday world' of initial teacher education: the contribution of micro-politics and critical social research' Unpublished paper, University of Warwick

Barker, M. (1981) *The New Racism*, London, Junction Books

Ben-Tovim, G., Gabriel, J., Law, I. and Stredder, K. (1986) *The Local Politics of Race*, London, Macmillan

Benhabib, Senla (1992) *Situating the Self: Gender, Community and Postmodernism*, Cambridge, Polity Press

Bennet, L. (1970) 'The challenge of blackness', *Black paper series,* Institute of the Black World publishers, April

Bhachu, P. (1991) 'Culture, ethnicity and class among Punjabi Sikh women in 1990s Britain', *New Community*, 17 (3) April, 401- 412

Bhopal, K. (1994) 'Asian women within the family: patriarchy or patriarchies?', Paper presented to British Sociological Association Annual Conference: 'Sexualities in Context, University of Central Lancashire, 28-31 March

Blase, J. (ed) (1991) *The Politics of Life in Schools: Power, Conflict and Co-operation*, London, Sage

Bourdieu, Pierre (1967) 'Systems of education and systems of thought', *Social Science Information*, 14, 338-58

Bourdieu, Pierre (1977) *Outline of a Theory of Practice*, Cambridge, Cambridge University Press

Bourdieu, Pierre (1981) 'Men and Machines', in: K. Knorr-Cetina and V. Cicourel (Eds) *Advances in Social Theory and Methodology: Towards an Integration of Micro and Macro-Sociologies*, London, Routledge and Kegan Paul

Bourdieu, Pierre (1983) 'The field of cultural production, or: The economic world reversed', *Poetics*, 12, 311-356

Bourdieu, Pierre (1984) *Distinction*, London, Routledge and Kegan Paul

Bourdieu, Pierre (1985a) 'The genesis of the concepts of Habitus and of Field', *Socio-criticism*, 2, 11-24

Bourdieu, Pierre (1985b) Social Space and the Genesis of Groups, *Theory and Society*, 14, 723-44

Bourdieu, Pierre (1987) What makes a Social Class? On the Theoretical and Practical Existence of Groups *The Berkeley Journal of Sociology*, 32, 1-17

Bourdieu, Pierre (1988) 'Vive la crise!: For heterodoxy in social science', *Theory and Society*, 17, 773-787

Bourdieu, Pierre (1990a) *The Logic of Practice*, Cambridge, Polity Press

Bourdieu, Pierre (1990b) *In Other words : Essays towards a Reflexive Sociology*, Cambridge, Polity Press

Bourdieu, Pierre (1990c) 'La domination masculine', *Actes de la recherche en sciences sociales*, 84, 2-31

Bourdieu, Pierre (1991) *The Craft of Sociology*, P. Bourdieu, J. Chamboredon and J. Passeron, New York, Walter de Gruyter

Bourdieu, Pierre (1992) *Language and Symbolic Power*, Cambridge, Polity Press

Bourdieu, P (1993a) 'Concluding Remarks: For a Sociogenetic Understanding of Intellectual Works', in: C. Calhoun, E. LiPuma and M. Postone (Eds) *Bourdieu: Critical Perspectives*, Cambridge, Polity Press

Bourdieu, Pierre (1993b) *La misere du monde*, Paris, Seuil

Bourdieu, Pierre (1993c) *Sociology in Question*, London, Sage

Bourdieu, Pierre and Passeron, J. (1977) *Reproduction in Education, Society and Culture*, London, Sage

Bourdieu, Pierre and Wacquant, L. (1992) *An Invitation to Reflexive Sociology*, Chicago, University of Chicago Press

Bourne J. and Sivanandan A. (1980) 'Cheerleaders and ombudsmen: the sociology of race relations in Britain', *Race and Class*, 21 (4) 331-52

Brah, Avtar and Minhas, Rehana (1985) 'Structural racism or cultural difference: schooling for Asian girls' in G. Weiner (ed) *Just a Bunch of Girls*, Milton Keynes, Open University Press

Brah, Avtar and Shaw, S. (1992) *Working Choices; South Asian young Muslim women and the labour market*, A report for the Department of Employment, research paper No. 91

Brannen J. (1988) 'Research note: the study of sensitive subjects', *Sociological Review,* 36 (3) 552-63

Brar H. S. (1992) 'Unasked questions, impossible answers, the ethical problems of researching race and education', in M. Leicester and M. Taylor, *Ethics, ethnicity and education*, London, Kogan Page

Brubaker, R. (1985) 'Rethinking Classical Sociology: The Sociological Vision of Pierre Bourdieu', *Theory and Society*, 14, 745-775

Brubaker, R. (1993) 'Social Theory as Habitus', in: C. Calhoun, E. LiPuma and M. Postone (Eds) *Bourdieu: Critical Perspectives*, Cambridge, Polity Press

Bryant, Beverley, Dadzie, Stella and Scafe, Suzanne (1985) *Heart of the Race: Black Women's Lives in Britain*, London, Women's Press

Buffond, Jean and Payne, Nellie (1990), *Jump-up-and-kiss-me: Two Stories from Grenada*, London, Women's Press

Cannon, Lynn, Higginbotham, Elizabeth and Leung, Marianne (1991) 'Race and class bias in qualitative research', in M. Fonow and J. Cook (Eds) *Beyond Methodology*, Bloomington, Indiana University Press

Carby Hazel (1982) 'White women listen! Black feminism and the boundaries of sisterhood' in Centre for Contemporary Cultural Studies *The Empire Strikes Back: Race and Racism in the 70s Britain,* London, Hutchinson

Carrington, Bruce (1983) 'Sport as a side-track: an analysis of West Indian involvement in extra-curricular sport', in: L. Barton and S. Walker (eds) *Race, Class and Education*, London, Croom Helm

Carrington, Bruce and Short, Geoffrey (1989) *'Race' and the Primary School: Theory into Practice*, Windsor, NFER-NELSON

Casey, K. (1994) *I Answer With My Life: Life Histories of Women Teachers Working for Social Change*, New York, Routledge

Centre for Contemporary Cultural Studies (1989) *The Empire Strikes Back: Race and Racism in 70' Britain*, London, Hutchinson

Chisholm, Lynne (1990) A Sharper Lens or a New Camera? Youth Research, Young People and Social Change in Britain. In Chisholm L, Buchner P, Kruger H-H, and Brown P (eds) *Childhood, Youth and Social Change: A Comparative Perspective*. Lewes, Falmer Press

Christian, B. (1989) 'But who do you really belong to, black studies or women's studies?', *Women's Studies*, 17, 17-23

Cicourel, A. V. (1993a) 'Aspects of Structural and Processual Theories of Knowledge', in: C. Calhoun, E. LiPuma and M. Postone (Eds) *Bourdieu: Critical Perspectives*, Cambridge, Polity Press

Cicourel, A. V. (1993b) 'Developmental and Adult Aspects of Habitus', in: von Gunter Gebaur und C. Wulf (Eds.) *Praxis und Asthetik: Neue Perspektiven im Denken Pierre Bourdieus,* Frankfurt am Main, Suhrkamp

Clarricoates, K. (1987) 'Child Culture at School: A Clash Between Gendered Worlds?' in A. Pollard (ed) *Children and Their Primary Schools,* Lewes, Falmer Press

Coard, Bernard (1971) *How the West Indian Child is made Educationally Sub-Normal by the British Education System,* London, Bogle L'Overture

Cohen L. and Manion L. (1989) *Research Methods in Education* (3rd edition), London, Routledge

Cohen, Philip (1988) 'The perversions of inheritance: studies in the making of multi-racist Britain', in: P. Cohen and H. Bains (eds) *Multi-Racist Britain,* London, Macmillan

Cohen, Philip (1992) '"It's racism what dunnit": hidden narratives in theories of racism', in: J. Donald and A. Rattansi (eds) *'Race', Culture and Difference,* London, Sage

Cohn, Tessa (1989) 'Sambo — a Study in Name Calling', In Kelly E and Cohn T (1988) *Racism in Schools — New Research Evidence,* Stoke, Trentham Books

Collins, M. (1987) *Angel, London, Women's Press*

Collins, Patricia Hill (1990), *Black Feminist Thoughts: Knowledge, Consciousness and the Politics of Empowerment: Perspectives on Gender* Vol 2 London, Routledge

Collins Patricia Hill (1991) 'Learning from the outsider within: the sociological significance of Black feminist thought' in M. Fonow and J. Cook (Eds) *Beyond Methodology,* Bloomington, Indiana University Press

Commission for Racial Equality (1986) *Black Teachers: The Challenge of Increasing the Supply. Report of a Residential Seminar,* London, CRE

Commission for Racial Equality (1988) *Medical School Admissions: Report of a formal investigation into St. George's Hospital Medical School,* London, CRE

Committee of Vice-Chancellors and Principles (1991) *Guidelines on Equal Opportunities in Higher Education,* Circulated document

Connell, (1987) *Gender and Power,* Cambridge, Polity Press

Connell, R.W. (1989) Cool guys, swots and wimps: The inter-play of masculinity and education, *Oxford Review of Education* 15 (3), 291-303

Connolly, Paul (1993) *Doing Feminist and Anti-Racist Research as a White Man: a contradiction in terms?* Paper presented to British Sociological Association Conference, Essex University

Connolly, Paul (1994) All lads together?: racism, masculinity and multicultural/anti-racist strategies in a primary school, *International Studies in Sociology of Education,* 4, 191-11

Connolly, Paul (1995a) Racism, masculine peer-group relations and the schooling of African/Caribbean infant boys, *British Journal of Sociology of Education,* 16 (2) pp. 75-92

Connolly, Paul (1995b) 'Boys will be boys?: Racism, sexuality and the construction of masculine identities amongst infant boys', in: J. Holland and M. Blair (eds) *Debates and Issues in Feminist Research and Pedagogy,* Clevedon, Multilingual Matters

Connolly, Paul (forthcoming) *Growing Up in the Inner City: Racism, Cultural Identities and the Primary School,* Buckingham, Open University Press

Cortazzi, Michael (1993) *Narrative Analysis,* Lewes, Falmer Press

Cotterill P. (1992) 'Interviewing women: issues of friendship, vulnerability and power', *Women's Studies International Forum,* 15 (5/6), 593-606

CRE (Commission for Racial Equality) (1988) *Learning in Terror.* London, CRE

Crozier, Gill (1994) 'Teachers' power, anti-racist education and the need for pupil involvement', *International Studies in Sociology of Education,* 4, 213-228

Davey, A. (1983) *Learning to be Prejudiced,* London, Edward Arnold

Davies, B. (1982) *Life in the Classroom and Playground,* London, Routledge and Kegan Paul

Davies, B. and Anderson, L. (1992) *Opting for Self-Management,* London, Routledge

Davis, Angela (1981) *Women, Race and Class,* London, Women's Press

Davis, L. (1987) 'Racism and sexism' In Delamont, S. (Ed) *The Primary School Teacher,* Lewes, Falmer Press

Deem, Rosemary; Brehoney, Kevin, J and Hemmings, Sue (1992) Social justice, social divisions and the governing of schools in D. Gill, B. Mayor and M. Blair (eds) *Racism and Education: Structures and Strategies,* London, Sage and the Open University

Delamont, Sarah (1989) *Knowledgeable Women,* London, Routledge

Denscombe, M., Szulc, H., Patrick, C. and Wood, A. (1986) Ethnicity and friendship: the contrast between sociometric research and fieldwork observation in primary school classrooms, *British Educational Research Journal,* 12, 3, 221-235

Denscombe, M. (1983) Ethnic Group and Friendship Choice in the Primary School, *Educational Research,* 25, 3, 184-190

Denzin, N. K. (1989) *Interpretive Biography,* London, Sage

Department of Education and Science (1985), *Report of the Committee of Inquiry into Education of Children from Ethnic Minority Groups,* London, HMSO

Di Maggio, P. (1979) 'Review Essay on Pierre Bourdieu', *American Journal of Sociology,* 84, 1460-74

Donald, James and Rattansi, Ali (eds.) (1992) *'Race', Culture and Difference,* London, Sage

Douglas, J.W.B. (1964) *The Home and the School,* London, MacGibbon and Kee

Du Bois B. (1983) 'Passionate scholarship: notes on values, knowing and method in feminist social science' in G. Bowles and R. Duelli Klein (Eds) Theories of Women's Studies, London, Routledge and Kegan Paul

Duelli Klein R. (1983) 'How do we do what we want to do: thoughts about feminist methodology' in G. Bowles and R. Duelli Klein (Eds) *Theories of women's studies,* London, Routledge and Kegan Paul

Eade, J. (1989) *The Politics of Community: the Bangladeshi Community in East London,* Aldershot, Gower

Edelman, M. (1964) *The Symbolic Use Of Politics,* Urbana: University of Illinois Press

Edelman, M. (1977) *Political Language: Words that Succeed and Policies that Fail,* New York, Academic Press

Edgell, Zee (1982), *Beka Lamb*, London, Heinemann

Edwards R. (1990) 'Connecting method and epistemology: a White woman interviewing Black women', *Women's Studies International Forum,* 13 (5), 477-490

Edwards R. (1993) 'An education in interviewing: placing the researcher and the research' in C. Renzetti and R. Lee (Eds), *Researching Sensitive Topics*, London, Sage

Eisner, E. (1993) 'Objectivity in Educational Research' in M. Hammersley, (ed) *Educational Research: Current Issues*, London, Paul Chapman Publishing

Engler, S. (1990) 'Illusory equality: The Discipline-based Anticipatory Socialisation of University Students', in: L. Chisholm, P. Buchner, H. Kruger and P. Brown (Eds) *Childhood, Youth and Social Change: A Comparative Perspective,* Lewes, Falmer Press

Epstein, Debbie (1993) *Changing Classroom Cultures: Anti-racism, Politics and Schools*, Stoke, Trentham Books

Erwin P (1993) *Friendship and Peer Relations in Children,* Chichester, John Wiley

Essed P. (1991) *Understanding Everyday Racism: An Interdisciplinary Theory*, London, Sage

Faulkner, J. (1991) 'Mixed-sex schooling and equal opportunities for girls : a contradiction in terms?' In *Research Papers in Education*, 16, 197-223

Finch J. (1984) 'It's great having someone to talk to: the ethics and politics of interviewing women', in C. Bell and H. Roberts (Eds) *Social Researching: Politics, Problems, Practice*, London, Routledge and Kegan Paul

Fine, G. A. (1987) *With the Boys: Little League Baseball and Preadolescent Culture*, Chicago, University of Chicago Press

Fonow, Mary Margaret and Cook, Judith A. (eds) (1991) *Beyond Methodology*, Bloomington, Indiana University Press

Forgacs, D. (ed) (1988) *A Gramsci Reader,* London, Lawrence and Wishart

Frankenberg, R. (1993) *The Social Construction of Whiteness: White Women, Race Matters*, London, Routledge

Freire, Paulo (1972) *Pedagogy of the Oppressed,* Harmondsworth, Penguin

Gallie, W. B. (1956) Essentially Contested Concepts, *Proceedings of the Aristotelian Society*, 56, 167-198

Gates, Henry Louis (1987) *Figures in Black: Words, Signs, and the 'Racial' Self*, Oxford University Press

Geertz, C. (1973) *The Interpretation of Cultures,* New York, Basic Books

Gelsthorpe L. (1992) Responses to Martyn Hammersley's paper 'on feminist methodology', *Sociology*, 26 (2), May 213-8

Gill, Dawn and Levidow, Les (eds) (1987) *Anti-racist Science Teaching,* Free Association Press

Gillborn, David (1990) *'Race', Ethnicity and Education,* London, Unwin and Hyman

Gillborn, David (1995) *Racism and Anti-Racism in Real Schools,* Open University Press

Gilroy Paul (1980) Managing the underclass: a further note on the sociology of race relations in Britain, *Race and Class*, 22 (1) 47-62

Gilroy Paul (1987) *There ain't no Black in the Union Jack*, London, Hutchinson

Gilroy, Paul (1990) The end of anti-racism, in W. Ball and J. Solomos (eds) *Race and Local Politics*, London, Macmillan

Gilroy, Paul (1992) 'Foreword', in B. Hesse, et al., *Beneath the Surface: Racial Harassment*, Aldershot, Avebury

Gilroy, Paul (1993) *Small Acts: Thoughts on the Politics of Black Cultures*, London, Serpents Tail

Gitlin, A., Siegel, M. and Boru, K. (1993) The Politics of Method: From Leftist Ethnography to Educative Research in M. Hammersley, (ed) *op. cit.*

Glucksmann M. (1994) The work of knowledge and knowledge of women's work, in M. Maynard and J. Purvis (Eds) *Researching Women's Lives from a Feminist Perspective*, London, Taylor and Francis

Goldberg D. (1993) *Racist Culture: Philosophy and the Politics of Meaning*, Oxford, Blackwell

Goodson, Ivor (ed) (1992) *Studying Teachers' Lives*, London, Routledge

Gouldner, A. (1979) *The Future of Intellectuals and the Rise of the New Class*, London, Macmillan

Graham, H. (1991) The concept of caring in feminist research: the case of domestic service, *Sociology*, 25 (1) Feb, 61-78

Green G., Barbour R., Barnard, M. and Kitinger J. (1993) Who wears the trousers?: Sexual harassment in research settings, *Women's Studies International Forum*, 16 (6) 627-637

Griffin, Christine (1987) Young women and the transition from school to unemployment: a cultural analysis in G. Weiner and M. Arnot (eds), *Gender under Scrutiny: New Enquiries in Education*, London, Hutchinson

Griffiths, Morwenna (1995a) Making a Difference: feminism, postmodernism and the methodology of educational research, *British Educational Research Journal*, 21 (2) 219-235

Griffiths, Morwenna (1995b) *Feminisms and the Self: The Web of Identity*, London, Routledge

Hage, G. (1994) Pierre Bourdieu in the nineties: Between the church and the atelier, *Theory and Society*, 23, 419-440

Hall, Stuart (1980) Race, articulation and societies structured in dominance. In UNESCO, *Sociological Theories: Race and Colonialism*, Paris, UNESCO

Hall, Stuart (1986) Gramsci's Relevance for the Study of Race and Ethnicity. *Communication Enquiry*, 10, 5-27

Hall, Stuart, Critcher C, Jefferson T, Clarke J and Roberts B (1978) *Policing the Crisis: Mugging, the State and Law and Order*, London, Macmillan

Hall, Stuart and Jefferson T (eds) (1976) *Resistance through Rituals: Youth Sub-cultures in Post-war Britain*, London, Hutchinson

Hall, Valerie (1994) Changing the subject: some methodological issues in studying gender and headship, Paper presented at the British Educational Research Association Annual Conference, Oxford University, September

Halsey, A.H. (1992) *Decline of the Donnish Dominion*, London, Clarendon Press

Hammersley, Martyn (1992) On feminist methodology, *Sociology*, 26 (2) May, 187-206

Hammersley, Martyn (ed) (1993) *Educational Research: Current Issues* London, Paul Chapman Publishing

Hammersley, Martyn and Atkinson, P. (1983) *Ethnography: Principles in Practice*, London, Tavistock

Handy, C. and Aitken, R. (1986) *Understanding Schools as Organisations*, Harmondsworth, Penguin

Harding, Jan (1986) *Perspectives on Gender and Science*, Lewes, Falmer Press

Harding, Sandra (1986) *The Science Question in Feminism*, Milton Keynes, Open University

Harding, Sandra (1987) *Feminism and Methodology*, Milton Keynes, Open University Press

Harding, Sandra (1991) *Whose Science? Whose Knowledge?* Milton Keyes, Open University Press

Harker, R., Mahar, C. and Wilkes, C. (1990) *An Introduction to the Work of Pierre Bourdieu: The Practice of Theory*, London, MacMillan

Hart C (ed) (1993) *Children on Playgrounds*, New York, State University of New York Press

Harvey L. (1990) *Critical Social Research*, London, Unwin Hyman

Hebidge, Dick (1982) *Subculture: The Meaning of Style*, London, Routledge

Herbert C. (1993) 'Researching adolescent girls' perceptions of unwanted sexual attention' in M. Kennedy, C. Lubelska and V. Walsh (Eds) *Making Connections*, London, Taylor and Francis

Hewitt, Roger (1986) *White Talk, Black Talk*, Cambridge, Cambridge University Press

Holland J. and Ramazanoglu C. (1994) Coming to conclusions: power and interpretation in researching young women's sexuality, in M. Maynard and J. Purvis (Eds) *Researching Women's Lives from a Feminist Perspective*, London, Taylor and Francis

hooks, bell (1982) *Ain't I A Woman?: Black Women and Feminism*, London, Pluto Press

hooks, bell (1992) *Black Looks: Race and Representation*, London, Turnaround

hooks, bell (1993) *Sisters of the Yam: Black Women and Self-recovery*, Boston MA, South End Press

hooks, bell (1993) Bell hooks speaking about Paulo Freire — The man his work, in McLaren, P. and Leonard, P. (Eds) *Paulo Freire: a Critical Encounter*, Routledge, London and New York

hooks, bell (1994) *Outlaw Culture: Resisting Representations*. London, Routledge

Horner, M. S. (1972) Towards an understanding of achievement related conflicts in women. *Journal of Social Issues*, 28, 157-75

Huber, L. (1990) Disciplinary Cultures and Social Reproduction, *European Journal of Education*, 25, 241-258

Jackson, Brian (1979) *Childminder*, London, Routledge

Jaggar, Alison (1983) *Feminist Politics and Human Nature,* Rowan and Littlefield

James, Comer P, and Poussaint, Alvin F (1992) *Raising Black Children,* Boston, Plumb Books

James Winston and Harris, Clive (eds.) (1993), *Inside Babylon: The Caribbean Diaspora in Britain,* London, Verso

Jeffers, S. (1991) Is race a sign of the times or is post-modernism only skin-deep? in M. Cross and M. Keith (Eds), *The City and the State,* London, Routledge

Jenkins, R. (1992) *Pierre Bourdieu,* London, Routledge

Jewson, N. and Mason, D. (1986) Theory and Practice of Equal Opportunities, *Sociological Review,* 34, 307-334

Jones, P. (1977) *An Evaluation of the Effect of Sport on the Integration of West Indian Schoolchildren,* Unpublished PhD Thesis, University of Surrey

Jones, Simon (1988) *White Youth, Black Culture: The Reggae Tradition from JA to UK,* Basingstoke, Macmillan

Kelly, Elinor (1988) Pupils, Racial Groups and Behaviour in Schools, in Kelly E and Cohn T, *Racism in Schools — New Research Evidence,* Stoke, Trentham Books

Kelly, Alison, (1987) (ed.) *Science for Girls,* Milton Keynes, Open University Press

Kenway, J., Willis, S., Blackmore, J. and Rennie, L. (1994) 'Making 'Hope Practical' Rather than 'Despair Convincing': feminist, post-structuralism, gender reform and educational change', *British Journal of Sociology of Education,* Vol.15, No.2, 187-210

Kelly L., Regan L. and Burton S. (1992) Defending the indefensible? Quantitative methods and feminist research, in H. Hinds, A. Phoenix and J. Stacey (eds), *Working Out: New Directions for Women's Studies,* London, Falmer Press

Kincaid, Jamaica (1985), *Annie John,* London, Pan Books

Kishwar M. (1994) A horror of isms, in M. Evans (ed) *The Woman Question* (second edition), London, Sage

Krais, B. (1993) Gender and Symbolic Violence: Female Oppression in the Light of Pierre Bourdieu's Theory of Social Practice, in: C. Calhoun, E. LiPuma and M. Postone (eds) *Bourdieu: Critical Perspectives,* Cambridge, Polity Press

Lamont, M. and Lareau, A. (1988) Cultural Capital: Allusions, Gaps and Glissandos in Recent Theoretical Developments, *Sociological Theory,* 6, 153-168

Lamont, M. (1992) *Money, Morals and Manners: The Culture of the French and American Upper-Middle Class,* Chicago, University of Chicago Press

Lather Patti (1986) 'Research as praxis' *Harvard Educational Review,* 56 (3), 257-277

Lawrence E. (1982) Just plain common sense: the 'roots' of racism, in Centre for Contemporary Cultural Studies, *The Empire Strikes Back: Race and Racism in 70s Britain,* London, Hutchinson

Lee, J. (1984) Contradictions and constraints in an inner city infant school, in G. Grace (ed.) *Education and the City: Theory, History and Contemporary Practice,* London, Routledge

LiPuma, E. (1993) Culture and the Concept of Culture in a Theory of Practice, in C. Calhoun, E. LiPuma and M. Postone (eds) *Bourdieu: Critical Perspectives*, Cambridge, Polity Press

Lorde, Audre (1994) Age, race, class and sex: women redefining difference, in M. Evans (ed) *The Woman Question* (second edition), London, Sage

Loveland, I. (1988) Discretionary Decision-Making in Housing Benefit Schemes: a case study, *Policy and Politics,* 16, 99-115

Lowenthal, B. (1994) Who's callin' who a bitch, *The Sunday Times* 8 Feb, p.12

Mac an Ghaill, Mairtin (1988) *Young, Gifted and Black: Student- Teacher Relations in the Schooling of Black Youth*, Milton Keynes, Open University Press

Mac an Ghaill Mairtin (1989) Beyond the White norm: the use of qualitative methods in the study of Black youths' schooling in England, *Qualitative Studies in Education*, 2 (3) 175-189

Mac an Ghaill, Mairtin (1990) 'State-school policy: contradictions, confusions and contestation' in *Journal of Education Policy,* (1991) 6, 299-313

Mac an Ghaill, Mairtin (1994) *The Making of Men: Masculinities, Sexualities and Schooling*, Buckingham, Open University Press

Macdonald, Ian, Bhavnani, Reena, Khan, Lily and John, Gus (1989) *Murder in the Playground: The Report of the Macdonald Inquiry into Racism and Racial Violence in Manchester Schools*, (The Burnage Report), London, Longsight Press

Mahar, C (1990) Pierre Bourdieu: The Intellectual Project, in: R Harker, C Mahar and C Wilkes (eds) *An Introduction to the Work of Pierre Bourdieu: The Practice of Theory*, London, MacMillan

Mama A. (1989) *The Hidden Struggle*, London, London Race and Housing Research Unit

Marshall A. (1994) Sensuous Sapphires: a study of the social construction of Black female sexuality, in M. Maynard and J. Purvis (eds) *Researching Women's Lives from a Feminist Perspective*, London, Taylor and Francis

Marshall, C. (ed) (1994) *The New Politics of Race and Gender*, Lewes, Falmer Press

Marshall, Paula (1982) *Brown Girl Brownstone*, London, Virago

May, S. (1994) *Making Multicultural Education Work,* Clevedon, Multilingual Matters

Maynard, Mary and Purvis, June (eds) *Researching Women's Lives from a Feminist Perspective*, London, Taylor and Francis

McClelland, Kathleen (1990) Culmative Disadvantage among the Highly Ambitious, *Sociology of Education*, 63, 102-121

McGurk H (ed) (1992) *Childhood Social Development,* Hove, Lawrence Erlbaum

Measor L. (1985) Interviewing: a strategy in qualitative research, in R.G. Burgess (ed), *Strategies of Educational Research: Qualitative Methods*, Lewes, Falmer Press

Mercer, Kobena (1994) *Welcome to the Jungle: New Positions in Black Cultural Studies*, London, Routledge

Middleton, S. (1992) Developing a Radical Pedagogy, in I. F. Goodson, (ed) *Studying Teachers' Lives*, London, Routledge

Mies, M. (1983) Towards a methodology for feminist research, in G. Bowles and R. Duelli Klein (eds) *Theories of women's studies*, London, Routledge and Kegan Paul

Miles, R. (1989) *Racism,* London, Routledge

Milner, David (1983) *Children and Race: Ten Years On*, London, Ward Lock

Mirza, Heidi (1992) *Young Female and Black*, London, Routledge

Mirza K. (1989) *The Silent Cry: Second Generation Bradford Muslim Young Women Speak*, Birmingham: Centre for the study of Islam and Christian-Muslim Relations

Morris, Jenny (1989) *Pride Against Prejudice: Transforming Attitudes to Disability*, London, Women's Press

Myers, Kate (1990) Review of *Equal Opportunities in the new ERA, Education,* 5 October, p.295

Neal, Sarah (1995) Researching Powerful People from Anti-Racist and Feminist Perspectives: a note on gender, collusion and marginality, *British Educational Research Journal,* 21, 4, 517-531

Neal, Sarah (1996) Deconstructing Equal Opportunities Discourses and Policies in Higher Education: two case studies, *Policy and Politics* (forthcoming)

Oakley, A. (1981) Interviewing women: a contradiction in terms, in H. Roberts (ed) *Doing Feminist Research*, London, Routledge

Oakley A. (1993) *Essays on women, medicine and health*, Cambridge, Cambridge University Press

Offe, C. (1984) *Contradictions of the Welfare State*, London, Hutchinson

Ollenburger J. and Moore H. (1992) *A Sociology of Women: The Intersection of Patriarchy, Capitalism and Colonisation*, London, Prentice Hall

Ouseley, Herman (1984) Local Authority Race Initiatives, in M. Boddy and C. Fudge (eds) *Local Socialism*, London, Macmillan

Ouseley, Herman (1990) Resisting Institutional Change, in J. Solomos and W. Ball (eds) *Race and Local Politics*, London, Macmillan

Parkin, F. (1964) *Middle Class Radicalism: The Social Bases of the British Campaign for Nuclear Disarmament*, Manchester, Manchester University Press

Parmar, Pratibha (1982) Gender, race and class: Asian women in resistance, in Centre for Contemporary Cultural Studies, *The Empire Strikes Back: race and racism in 70s Britain*, London, Hutchinson

Parmar, Pratibha (1990) Black feminism: the politics of articulation, in Jonathon Rutherford (ed) *Identity: Community, Culture, Difference*, London, Lawrence and Wishart

Peacock, A. (1991) (ed) *Science in Primary Schools: the multicultural dimension*, London, Macmillan

Peterson-Lewis, Sonja (1991) A feminist analysis of the defenses of obscene rap lyrics, in J. M. Spencer (ed), *The Emergence of Black and the Emergence of Rap*, North Carolina, Duke University Press.

Phoenix, Ann (1994a) Practising feminist research: the intersection of gender and 'race' in the research process, in M. Maynard and J. Purvis (eds) *Researching Women's Lives from a Feminist Perspective,* London, Taylor and Francis

Phoenix, Ann (1994b) Narrow definitions of culture: the case of early motherhood, in M. Evans (ed) *The Woman Question* (second edition), London, Sage

Phoenix, Ann (1987) Theories of gender and black families, in G. Weiner and M. Arnot (eds) *Gender Under Scrutiny: New Inquiries in Education*, London, Unwin Hyman

Pollard, Andrew (1985) *The Social World of the Primary School*, London, Holt, Rinehart and Winston

Pollard, Andrew (1990) Towards a Sociology of Learning in Primary Schools, in *British Journal of Sociology of Education*, 11, 241- 256

Quicke, J. and Winter, C. (1994) Teaching the Language of Learning: towards a metacognitive approach to pupil empowerment, in *British Educational Research Journal*, 20, 429-445

Ramazanoglu, Caroline (1992) On feminist methodology: male reason versus female empowerment, *Sociology*, 26 (2), May, 207-212

Raphael Reed, Lynn (1995) *Working with Boys*, unpublished research supported through a research fellowship (1995-1998) at the Faculty of Education, University of the West of England, Bristol

Rattansi, Ali (1992) Changing the subject? Racism, culture and education, in J. Donald and A. Rattansi (eds) *'Race', Culture and Difference,* London, Sage

Rattansi, Ali and Reeder, D. (eds) (1992) *Rethinking Radical Education,* London, Lawrence and Wishart

Reay, Diane (1991) Intersections of Gender, Race and Class in the Primary School, *British Journal of Sociology of Education,* 12, 163-182

Reay, Diane (1995 forthcoming) They employ cleaners to do that: Habitus in the primary classroom, *British Journal of Sociology of Education*, 6

Reed, M. and Beveridge, M. (1993) 'Knowing Ourselves: practising a pluralist epistemology in teacher education' in C. Reissman (1987) 'When gender isn't enough: women interviewing women', *Gender and Society,* 1 (2), June 172-207

Reid, M. (1983) A feminist sociological imagination? Reading Ann Oakley, *Sociology of Health and Illness*, 5 (1), 83-94

Renzetti, C. and Lee, R. (eds)*, Researching Sensitive Topics*, London, Sage

Reynolds G. (1993) 'And Gill came tumbling after': gender, emotion and a research dilemma, in M. Kennedy, C. Lubelska and V. Walsh (eds) *Making Connections*, London, Taylor and Francis

Rhodes, P. J. (1994) Race of interviewer effects in qualitative research: a brief comment, *Sociology*, 28 (2), 547-558

Ribbens, J. (1989) Interviewing — an 'unnatural situation'?, *Women's Studies International Forum*, 12 (6), 579-592

Richardson, Robin (1992) Race policies and programmes under attack: two case studies for the 1990s, in D Gill, B Mayor and M Blair (eds) *Racism and Education: Structures and Strategies*, London, Sage and the Open University

Riddell, S. (1992) *Gender and the politics of the curriculum*, London, Routledge

Riddell, S. (1992) 'Gender and Education: progressive and conservative forces in the balance' in S. Brown and S. Riddell (eds) *Class, Race and Gender in Schools*, Scottish Council for Research in Education, Publication 113, Edinburgh, SCRE

Risseeuw, C. (1991) Bourdieu, Power and Resistance: Gender Transformation in Sri Lanka, in: Kathy Davis (ed) *The Gender of Power*, London, Sage

Rizvi, Fazal (1994) Race, gender and the cultural assumptions of schooling, in C. Marshall (ed.) *The New Politics of Race and Gender*, Lewes, Falmer

Rizvi, Fazal (1993) Critical introduction: researching racism and education, in B. Troyna (ed) *Racism and Education*, Buckingham, Open University

Robbins, D (1991) *The Work of Pierre Bourdieu*, Oxford, Oxford University Press

Roberts, H. (ed) (1981) *Doing Feminist Research*, London, Routledge

Robinson, V. (1986) *Transients, Settlers and Refugees: Asians in Britain*, Oxford, Clarendon press

Ross, Carol et al. (1990) *'Can I stay in Today Miss?': Improving the school playground*, Stoke on Trent, Trentham

Rutherford, J. (1990) A place called home, in J. Rutherford (eds) *Identity, Community, Culture and Difference*, London, Lawrence and Wishart

Scanlon J. (1993) Challenging the imbalances of power in feminist oral history, *Women's Studies International Forum*, 16 (6) 639-645

Seiber J. E. (1993) The ethics and politics of sensitive research, in C. Renzetti and R. Lee (eds), *Researching Sensitive Topics*, London, Sage

Sewell, W, H (1992) The Theory of Structure: Duality, Agency, and Transformation, *American Journal of Sociology*, 98 no 1 pp.1-29

Shackleton, J. (1993) USA Community Colleges and Further Education in Britain, *Oxford Studies Comparative Education*, 3,

Shantz, C. U. and Hartup, W. W. (eds) (1992) *Conflict in Child and Adolescent Development*, Cambridge, Cambridge University Press

Shor, I. and Freire, P. (1987) *A Pedagogy for Liberation*, New York, Bergin and Garvey

Sivanandan, A. (1985) RAT and the degradation of the black struggle, *Race and Class* 26 (4) 1-34

Skellington, R. (1992) *'Race' in Britain Today*, London, Sage

Sluckin, A. (1981) *Growing Up in the Playground*, London, Routledge

Smart, Carol (1984) *The Ties that Bind: Law, Marriage and the Reproduction of Patriarchal Relations*, London, Routledge and Kegan Paul

Solomos, John (1983) *The Politics of Black Youth Unemployment*, Working Papers on Ethnic Relations, No.20 Research Unit on Ethnic Relations, Aston University

Solomos, John and Back, Les (1994) Conceptualising racisms: social theory, politics and research *Sociology*, 28 (1) pp.143-161

Stacey J. (1988) Can there be a feminist ethnography?, *Women's Studies International*, 11 (1), 21-27

Stanley, Liz and Wise, Sue (1993) *Breaking Out Again* (second edition), London, Routledge

Stanley, Liz and Wise, Sue (1990) *Feminist Praxis*, London, Routledge

Staples, Robert (1982) *Black Masculinity: The Black Man's Role in American Society*, San Francisco, Black Scholar Press.

Szczelkun, S (1993) *The Conspiracy of Good Taste*. (London, Working Press)

Tanna, K. (1987) *The experiences of South Asian university students in the British education system and in their search for work*, Unpublished thesis, University of Aston

Thorne, B. (1993) *Gender Play*. Buckingham, Open University Press

Times Educational Supplement Lost for words in an unequal world, 9 September 1994

Times Educational Supplement Baffled contestants in the regeneration game, 14 October 1994

Tomlinson, Sally (1984) *Home and School in Multicultural Britain*, London, Batsford Academic

Tong, R. (1989) *Feminist Thought: A Comprehensive Introduction*, Sydney, Unwin and Hyman

Troyna, Barry (1993a) *Racism and Education: Research Perspectives*, Buckingham, Open University Press

Troyna, Barry (1993b) *Sounding a Discordant Note? 'Being Critical' and 'Critical Beings' in Education Policy Research*. Paper presented to 5th Cambridge International Conference on Educational Evaluation, University of Cambridge

Troyna, B. and Carrington Bruce (1993) 'Whose side are we on? Ethical dilemmas in research on 'race' and education', in B. Troyna (ed) *Racism and Education*, Buckingham, Open University Press

Troyna, Barry and Hatcher, Richard (1992) *Racism in Children's Lives: A study of Mainly-white Primary Schools*, London, Routledge

Troyna, Barry and Williams, J. (1986) *Racism, Education and the State*, London, Croom Helm

van Dijk T (1987) *Communicating Racism*, Newbury Park, Sage

Verma, Gajendra (ed) *Inequality and Teacher Education: An International Perspective*, Lewes, Falmer Press

Walden, Rosie and Walkerdine, Valerie (1985) *Girls and Mathematics: From Primary to Secondary Schooling*, University of London, Bedford Way Papers

Walkerdine, Valerie (1988) *The Mastery of Reason: Cognitive Development and the Production of Rationality*, London, Routledge

Walkerdine, Valerie (1990) *Schoolgirl Fictions*, Verso, London, New York

Wallace, Mike and McMahon, Agnes (1994) *Planning for Change in Turbulent Times* London, Cassell

Wambu, Onyekachi (1994) Inner Vision, *The Voice*, 11 Oct, p.6

Warren C. (1988) *Gender issues in field research*, (9) London, Sage

Weiler, Kathleen (1988) *Women Teaching for Change: gender, class and power*, Boston, Bergin and Garvey

Weiner, Gaby (1994) *Feminisms in Education: an introduction*, Open University Press, Buckingham

Weiner, Gaby (1992*)* Staffing Policies in Further and Higher Education: setting the scene. Paper presented in the Equal Opportunities in Management symposium, CEDAR International Conference, Warwick University

Weiner, Gaby, Farish, M., Powney, J. and McPake, J. (1995) *Increasing Equality in Further and Higher Education: Towards Better Practices,* Buckingham, Open University Press

Weis, L. (1992) Reflections on the researcher in a multi-cultural environment, in C. Grant (ed) *Research and Multi-cultural Education*, Lewes, Falmer Press

Werbner, P. (1990) *The Migration Process: Capital Gifts and Offerings Among British Pakistanis*, Oxford, Berg

Williams, Jenny (1985) Redefining institutional racism, *Ethnic and Racial Studies* 8, 3, 323-348

Williams, Jenny (1987) The construction of women and black students as educational problems, in M. Arnot and G.Weiner (eds) *Gender and the Politics of Schooling*, London, Hutchinson

Williams, Jenny, Cocking, J., and Davies, L. (1989) *Words or Deeds: a review of Equal Opportunity Policies in Higher Education*, London, Commission for Racial Equality

Willis, Paul (1983) Cultural Production and Theories of Reproduction. In L. Barton and S. Walker (eds) *Race, Class and Education,* London, Croom Helm

Wolpe, A. (1988) *Within School Walls: the Role of Discipline, Sexuality and the Curriculum,* London, Routledge

Woods, Peter (1980) *Pupil Strategies,* London, Croom Helm

Wright, Cecile (1992) *Race Relations in the Primary School*, London, David Fulton

Wright, Cecile (1987) The Relations Between Teachers and Afro-Caribbean Pupils: Observing Multi-racial Classrooms, in G. Weiner and M. Arnot (eds) *Gender Under Scrutiny*, London, Hutchinson

Subject Index

ANTIRACISM, CULTURE AND SOCIAL JUSTICE IN EDUCATION

Name Index

Clark, D. 179
Clarke, J. 98
Clarricoates, K. 99
Coard, B. 154
Cockburn, C. 3
Cocking, J. 2, 3, 154
Cohen, P. 131, 133
Cohn, T. 97
Collins, M. 152, 154,
Collins, P.H. 104, 150, 167, 168, 176, 180
Commission for Racial Equality 1, 2
Committee of Vice-Chancellors and Principles 2
Connell, R.W. 34, 35, 46
Connolly, P. 5, 133, 138, 141, 147, 166
Cortazzi, M. 78
Cotterill, P. 104, 180
Critcher, C. 98
Crozier, O. 84, 85, 134
Dadzie, S. 150, 154, 180
Daley, M. 30
Davey, A. 97
Davies, B. 94, 99
Davies, L. 2, 3, 51, 154
Davies, A. 134
Deem, R. xviii, xix
Delamont, Sarah 116
Denscombe, M. 99
Denzin, N. K. 79
Derrida, J. 22
Di Maggio, P. 120
Douglas, J.W.B. 76
Du Bois, B. 181
Duelli Klein, R. 181
Eade, J. 63
Edelman, M. 6, 7
Edgell, Z. 152
Edwards, R. 103, 170, 176, 177, 179, 181

Eisner, E. 80
Engler, S. 116
Epstein, D. 93
Erwin, P. 99
Fanon, F. 22
Farish, M. 3
Faulkner, J. 45
Finch, J. 173, 176, 177, 181
Fine, C. A. 99
Forgacs, D. 100
Foster, P. 39
Foucault, M. 40
Freire, P. 82
Fuller, M. 40
Gabriel, J. 18, 166
Gallie, W. B. 6
Gates, H. L. 31
Geertz, C. 80
Gelsthorpe, L. 104, 180
Gill, D. 152
Gillborn, D. 3, 39, 133, 134
Gilroy, P. xvii, xix, 2, 4, 7, 30, 37, 133
Gitlin, A. 80
Glucksmann, M. 179
Goldberg, D. 2, 166
Goodson, Ivor 80
Gottman, J. M. 99
Gouldner, A. 2
Gramsci, 100
Green, G. 171
Griffin, C. 62
Griffiths, M. 46, 153
Hage, G. 121
Hall, S. xvii, 21, 98, 100
Haldane 179
Halsey, A.H. 2
Hammersley, M. 62, 79
Handy, C. 9
Harding, J. 152
Harding, S. 181